# OF SWEDISH WAYS

# OF SWEDISH WAYS

BY LILLY LORÉNZEN

ILLUSTRATED BY DICK SUTPHEN

GRAMERCY PUBLISHING COMPANY
New York

This 1986 edition is published by Gramercy Publishing Company,
distributed by Crown Publishers, Inc., 225 Park Avenue South,
New York, New York 10003, by arrangement with Dillon Press.

Printed and Bound in the United States of America

**Library of Congress Cataloging-in-Publication Data**

Lorénzen, Lilly.
  Of Swedish ways.

  Bibliography: p. 275.
  1. Sweden—Social life and customs.  I. Title.
DL631.L6   1986        948.5         86-3129
ISBN 0-517-60555-4

h g f e d c b a

# CONTENTS

# SWEDEN
## SVERIGE

Lappland

Norrbotten

Västerbotten

Jämtland

Ångermanland

Härjedalen

Medelpad

Hälsingland

**SVERIGE**

Dalarna

Gästrikland

Värmland

Västmanland

Uppland

Dalsland

Närke

Södermanland

Bohuslän

Västergötland

Östergötland

Gottland

Halland

Småland

Öland

Skåne

Blekinge

# A SALUTE

It has been said, "What the son takes pains to forget the grandson seeks to remember." The later generations of the Swedish-Americans have become aware of, even curious, about their heritage and desire to know more about it. Often a Swedish-born grandmother's actions seemed odd to her American grandchildren. Why did she choose to settle an argument by quoting a proverb? Why did she insist on celebrating Christmas on the Eve of Christmas? Why did she accord such importance to Midsummer?

This book attempts to answer questions like these. It attempts to explain something of what makes up the Swedish heritage and perhaps in some way contribute to a greater understanding of a culture that is paradoxical, steeped as it is in ancient, earthy rituals and observations on one hand and embracing modern concepts and attitudes on the other. For obvious reasons it offers little that is new to any one who was born into the Swedish culture and schooled in its traditions, and it does not deal with the development of Sweden of today. It deals rather with an earlier Swedish way of life, looked at with a backward glance. It simply lends an ear to voices from the past in the attempt to clarify the meaning and import of Sweden's agelong customs and traditions.

To most Americans of Swedish descent the name

*Sverige* (Sweden) made an early impression. You heard
it as a child and wondered perhaps what kind of place
it was, or what it meant to be *svensk* (Swedish). On the
other hand it might well be that you did not ponder the
matter at all for the reason that every family in your community was Swedish. Your mother looked like all the
other women with her hair combed up into a bun on top
of her head, and your father looked like any other man—
perhaps more handsome than the rest, as you remember
him. When all the grown-ups got together they spoke the
same language. It was Swedish. Perhaps you learned to
understand such expressions as *sitt still, tacka nu för
maten, nu ska vi gå hem,* even if you did not know the
words singularly.

It was not until you were an adult that you formed a
definite concept of what *Sverige* was. If your parents had
come from wretched homes you naturally imbibed their
bitter memories and you dwelled on how fortunate it was
that you did not have to grow up in such misery. An entirely different view was yours had your parents enjoyed
a happy childhood in Sweden. Nostalgia colored their
comments and you became part of a conscious loyalty.

But regardless of the background of your parents and
grandparents you have inherited some Swedish traits and
these qualities continue to influence the course of your
life as they influence the part you play in the community.
As each nationality that is represented in the United States
tries to give of its best to the American way of life, so do
you try to contribute of your best to it. In the belief that
Swedish ways still mean something to those who have inherited them, this book was written.

Knowing that a younger generation is searching to
know more about these Swedish ways I am delighted to
dedicate the book to all those many students who, hearing

some of the answers to the questions on the subject in my class room at the University of Minnesota and at the American Swedish Institute in Minneapolis, have urged me to write them down so they would not be lost to future generations.

To all other Americans who have the Swedish heritage at heart I extend my dedication.

L. L.

**HEMBYGD**

# HEMBYGD

What is *hembygd*? One gropes for a satisfactory word in English and fumbles with hometown, birthplace, home farm, but gives up in mild frustration. The first part of the word is home, of course, and the second part involves the area around the home. Therefore, *hembygd* can mean region, neighborhood, or countryside.

Verner von Heidenstam (1859-1940), author, member of the Swedish Academy, and Nobel prize winner in 1916, has described it from the core. "At home—you also have pondered the word. You have repeated it quietly to yourself—at home, at home! It begins as the child counts the nails and knotholes in the floor boards. At home—it is something that begins with a small seed and results in a large tree. It begins with the nursery, and it grows and becomes several rooms and a whole house, a whole area, a whole country. And outside that country even the air and the water loses its refreshing fragrance." This sentiment is reflected in the nostalgic lines written during the author's stay abroad. "Jag längtar hem sen åtta långa år. . . . Jag längtar marken, jag längtar stenarna där barn jag lekt." (For eight long years he had longed for home . . . the ground, even the rocks where he had played as a child.)

Another member of the Swedish Academy and Nobel prize winner in 1951 is the contemporary author Pär Lagerkvist (1891-    ) who expresses his deep feeling of

attachment to the place of childhood memories in the
following lines from *Sång och strid, 1940* (Song and Strife)
called *"Detta är landet"* (This Is the Land):

> "Det slitna stället på hemmets grind
> Som nötts genom åren av händer
> Som väl jag kände, och gårdens lind
> Som doft ner mot vägen sänder,
> Det är mig kärt, ej jag älskar så
> Något annat som finns i världen.
> En gång som död skall jag längta att stå
> Vid grinden bland hemmets gärden."

An attempt to reshape poetry into another word
pattern is almost bound to fail. On the other hand, a great
man's expression of thoughts can be made accessible in
prose, too. Here is the attempt:

The smooth, shiny place on the gate at home which has
become worn by hands that I knew well, and the linden
tree in the yard which is sending forth its fragrance down
the road—all is dear to me. Nothing in the world do I
love more than that. Once when I am dead I shall yearn
to stand by the gate amidst the fields at home.

When still in the bosom of home and not yet having
stirred far away from it we take its solid ground and fixed
whereabouts for granted. "Is there anything else?" seemed
to be the attitude of a Värmland lad standing idle at a
street corner in Sunne one lovely summer evening when a
couple of tourists approached him and inquired about a
place where they could have a good dinner. He looked
puzzled, pushed his shapeless cap further down the back
of his head and said: "Dä vet ja' int'—ja' äter hemme." (I
don't know—I eat at home.)

For many individuals home is where you hang your
hat. To others home is not merely four walls but a castle
where security and affection dwell. The early Swedish

settler in America wanted more than anything to establish a home. He was willing to work hard for it, and when he found even a small place that he could call his own he felt rewarded. Nostalgia tugged at his heart, surely, but pride kept him moving ahead. And soon his new surroundings became home to him, and in time he himself fitted into the fascinating puzzle game that made up the colorful picture of the new world called America. He gave not only new strength and working power to the young growing nation but also those qualities of head and heart that made up his cultural heritage.

*Hemlängtan* is a telling word that does not very well lend itself to translation. In earlier days it was a word not as often spoken as it was felt. It was a feeling of nostalgia, longing, pining for home, sometimes even described as suffering. There was not much in the new surroundings that looked like home to the new settlers. The one object that spelled out *hembygd* more than any other was the chest that had accompanied them to the new world. It had an honored place in the meagerly furnished cabin, and was referred to as *Amerika-kistan*. It had been taken out for the long voyage across the sea from the shed or attic where it had been standing for a long time covered with dust and cobweb. Yes, it was sturdily built. Scrubbed and cleaned it had taken on a new look. Perhaps the initials of the original owner and the year when it was made still were visible. Who could the owner have been? In most cases it was soon established that a grandmother had received the chest as her *brudkista* (bridal chest) where she later had kept her parish costume, for instance, and grandfather's Sunday vest, her fine pieces of linen and woolens, and the first child's baptismal gown. It spelled out home to a Swedish settler. He treasured it, and today his grandchildren, or great grandchildren in this country have learned to treasure it. If only such a chest could talk. . . .

It is only natural that the first generation of Swedish settlers in America lived by their inherited traditions and that they conveyed to their children the Swedish ways and customs. While they groped for contacts with the new world and for strange new English words, learned by snatches, they still spoke Swedish among themselves. And to many of their children this was the only language they knew until they began school and were required to learn English. The concepts of one child growing up in these new surroundings were written down by Anna Olsson in her book *En prärieunges funderingar* (Reflections of a Youngster from the Prairie). As the young daughter of a Swedish clergyman she did ponder and she did observe what took place around her. The following are a few samples of her observations, the first being a notion of what a conference is:

"Det kom så många präster, och mississar med. Och de provpredikade i kyrkan var sin gång, och sedan sitter de och talar med varandra. Och när det är slut i kyrkan så går de hem och röker och röker, så de röker. Det heter konferens . . .

"Värmland är den roligaste plats som finns på jorden. I Värmland växer det många vackra blommor, vitsippor och blåsippor och liljekonvalje. Och prästkragar! Pappa har en prästkrage på sig när han predikar i kyrkan . . .

"Pappa har lovat Gerda och mig var sin psalmbok, om vi inte dricker kaffe ända till jul . . .

"Farmor har sett den Onde. Han är ful och lång och mager, längre än trädtopparna i skogen. Farmor sa: 'Gå din väg, fuling!' När han inte gav sig iväg tog farmor fram bibeln och då blev han rädd och sprang."

In translation the appealing, guileless simplicity of the

original text is apt to get lost, but here is an attempt:

So many ministers came, and their Mrs.'s, too. And in turn they gave their probationary sermons in church, and after that they sit and talk with one another. And when it is over in church they go home (as guests in her home, evidently) and smoke and smoke—how they smoke. That is called a conference.

The place on earth where it is most fun to be is Värmland (the province from which the family had emigrated). Many beautiful flowers grow in Värmland —white and blue anemones and lilies of the valley. And daisies! (The Swedish word can mean both daisy and clerical collar.) Papa has a clerical collar on when he preaches in church.

Papa has promised Gerda and me each a hymnbook, if we do not drink coffee until Christmas.

Grandmother has seen the devil (the Evil One). He is ugly and tall and thin, taller than the tree tops in the forest. Grandmother said: "Go away, you beast!" When he did not budge, grandmother brought out the Bible and then he became frightened and ran.

"THE OLD COUNTRY"

# "THE OLD COUNTRY"

The emigrating Swede called his native land *det gamla landet*—the old country—and often his nostalgic thoughts would recall the small cottage where he was born, the road into town, the red school house flanked with birch trees. Whatever the birthplace a tall, lovely birch was often held in fond memory. Perhaps as a young boy he had carved his initials in its trunk. He remembered how it looked in the winter time when the hoarfrost outlined every branch and twig and it stood there like a stiff bouquet in white, and he visualized how it appeared when the soft branches trembled and swayed in the summer breeze. Had he lived in the depths of Norrland, the northern part of Sweden, he recalled the dark, dense forest of pine and spruce, and he longed for the heady scent of pitch and pine cones in his nostrils. And all Swedes remembered well their blue shimmering lakes.

Sweden is said to have 96,000 lakes. Together with the many rivers they comprise 8.6 per cent of the total area of the country which is 173,630 square miles. It ranks fourth among the European countries and compared with a given area in the United States it comes out slightly larger than California, for instance. Sweden is a long and narrow country, about 1,000 miles in length and about 350 miles across its widest part. The population as of January 1, 1970 was 8,012,000.

Going from south to north, the three main regions of
Sweden are Götaland, Svealand, and Norrland. These in
turn are divided into provinces, called *landskap*. Most
Swedish-Americans know some of the names, such as
Värmland, Dalarna, Västergötland, Östergötland, Småland, Halland, Skåne, Blekinge, Dalsland, Bohuslän. In
this country devotion to the province where one was born,
or from where one's parents or grandparents came, becomes a matter of personal attachment and loyalty, and
a number of clubs and societies cultivate this feeling of
kinship. In Sweden, this emotional response is more diffuse,
that is, with a few exceptions. People from Dalarna, for
instance, have an age-long devotion to their native province. A *dalmas* (male inhabitant) lives close to the soil,
tilled by his forefathers before him, and he adheres to
traditions. His inborn independence is reflected in his
bearing, his straightforward approach to strangers. He is
quick-witted, always ready with a joke. He is often skillful
with a fiddle. It is said that there is not a home in Dalarna
that does not have a violin, frequently homemade. It might
be hidden in a closet, or proudly displayed on the wall,
but it is used and revered. In their picturesque dress,
fiddlers are welcome guests at wedding feasts and funerals
alike, lending added color and festivity to the former, and
relieving the latter of the deep somberness usually en-
veloping black-garbed mourners in Sweden.

Dalarna is the last stronghold of the native costume, and
this is particularly true of the villages around Lake Siljan,
such as Leksand, Rättvik, and Mora. In church on Sundays
one will find the inhabitants dressed in their parish costumes, the women wearing their colorful, striped aprons
which differ in pattern from parish to parish. Although
the custom is slowly giving way to modern attire, it is
strictly observed at midsummer when young and old don

their native dress. Tourists gather from near and far to look at and to photograph the festive crowd dancing around the maypole, and to buy the stiff-legged, gaily painted Dala-horse as a souvenir. He even finds his way to distant lands and is known to attract business for an inn or restaurant in the United States where he stands, large and imposing, at the entrance beckoning the hungry to come in and taste a Swedish meal. The fastidious guardians of Swedish art and culture may wish that the interests and inclinations of tourists could be guided into channels offering more genuine Dala-traditions.

Woodcraft products in general have for generations demonstrated the inbred skill of the Dala-people. Carving of toys for children, such as horses, birds, and dolls was a common occupation in farm homes as well as in the woodsmen's temporary quarters during the long winter evenings. When in times of poor crops it became necessary to augment the income with revenues from other sources, these items were sold in neighboring provinces, proving a profitable commodity.

The work of painting and decorating the carved pieces was left to those families who had developed a special skill in so called *krusning*. In Mora parish today the people of the Nisser farm (Nissergården) have earned this distinction. The characteristic motif is a flourish of swirling lines and broad strokes in bright colors.

With a wagon load of painted horses and other home-produced articles, such as bright ribbons, casks, barrels, handwoven materials, and copper pots, the Dala-men would venture out to sell and to barter in exchange for grain. After staying overnight on farms along the way, they would upon departure offer a painted horse or two to the children as a token of appreciation for their lodging. Stories are told how they journeyed far and managed well without

ready cash and how one such traveler, commonly called
*Silen,* succeeded in obtaining free lodging altogether. He
was believed to be on the devil's errand and fear gripped
the farm people whenever he drove into their yard. When
he left the next morning without bestowing a gift, they
were only too glad to have him out of sight. Another Dala-
man known for his ready wit came at one time with a full
load of painted horses to a merchant in Morastrand, who
refused to buy them. Times were such, he complained, that
it was not possible to sell anything. "Don't despair," the
tradesman said, "as long as the cradle will rock, you'll
need toy horses in stock." The load was accepted.

Dalarna, often called the heart of Sweden, casts its spell
over those living there, and whenever they depart for other
lands a bit of their own hearts is bound to be left there.
Visitors come under the spell, too. As Hans Christian Andersen (1805-1875), the Danish author of fairy tales,
wrote after a visit in 1849: "Painters and poets, join hands
and go to Dalarna! This country is rich in beauty and
poetry and richest around Lake Siljan."

On the other hand, could anyone be more loyal to his
province than an inhabitant of Skåne, the southernmost
part of Sweden? The lyric lines: *Väl gläds jag att heta
svensk ibland, men jag yvs att vara skåning!* tell the story.
It means that he is happy to be Swedish—at times—but he
glories in being born in Skåne! And justified he might be,
for the land is rich and fertile and the grain grows higher
there and harvests are more abundant than in any other
part of the country. It follows that food is an item of
importance, as the old saying reveals: *Go mad och möen
mad och mad i rättan tid,* that is, good food and much
food and food at the proper time. His girth grows, too, it is
said, although such generalizations must be made with cau-
tion. On the other hand, old sayings are not taken out of

thin air, so at some time or other there might very well have lived one or two or more jovial, rotund Skåne farmers who with evident enjoyment gave themselves over to eating and thus happened to find a way into the folklore of the province. And in Skåne today, the habit of good eating lives on. A feast of special importance is the goose dinner eaten on Saint Mårten's day, the eleventh of November. The legend of Saint Mårten, who died on that day in the year 400, tells how the pious prelate at one time took refuge in a goose pen when members of his diocese insisted on making him a bishop. The loud cackling of the geese revealed his whereabouts, however, and much against his will Mårten was installed as bishop. But he could not forget who caused him to yield. Death unto the geese, he ordered, and ever since the people of Skåne have slaughtered and eaten goose on Saint Mårten's day.

Another legend deals with Småland and how it came into being. Our Lord, the story goes, was occupied with the creation of Skåne, making it the luscious land it is, and directed Saint Peter to bring order to the piece of land north of it. Saint Peter went to work, but he felt he did not have much to do with. He began, however, by placing a layer of soil on the multitude of rocks and stone formations and planting pine and spruce and birch between the streams and the lakes. When finished he was quite proud of his work. But before Our Lord had a chance to come and inspect it, a heavy rainstorm washed away the soil and made bare the long stretches of rocks and boulders in the ground. Saint Peter was in despair. When Our Lord saw the stony, meager ground he rebuked his helper. "I have just created a rich, fruitful land to the south," he said. "Go forth and create men to live in it. Mine shall be a harder task here." So Saint Peter went away and Our Lord created the *smålänning* and made him strong and ambitious, stubborn and shrewd, and He called the land "Småland" because the tillable pieces were so small. And ever since it has been said about the *smålänning* that even if he is placed on a rock at sea he will find a way of livelihood.

So far the legend. How does it coincide with reality? As far as the stony ground is concerned it has been there ever since creation. In part it is still there today. But most of the loose rocks have been removed and gathered into neat stone fences around small patches of land. In order to get even a small piece of soil cleared, the strong, hard working Småland farmer had to carry away the heavy stones with his bare hands, and it is said that his arms grew longer and longer as he worked at it. Farming was more or less an endurance test. In all too many cases it failed to give the farmer even a meager subsistence. By the middle of the nineteenth century stories began to reach the poor Småland farmer concerning America, the wondrous country where there were wide stretches of land to be had with soil so rich and fertile that seed sprouted almost as soon as. it touched the ground. He owed it to his family to try his luck. One family after another began the trek to the Middle West and in most cases they headed for Minnesota. The descendants of these Småland families now live in Lindstrom, Center City, Chisago City, and other towns in the state. In his monumental work in four volumes, entitled *The Emigrants, Unto a Good Land, The Settlers,* and *The Last Letter Home,* the Swedish novelist Vilhelm Moberg (1898-    ) tells the story of the emigrating *smålänning* and how he fared in the new country.

Surely, each province in Sweden has its story. Who can tell more vivid tales than the people from Värmland, the province of lyricism, where imagination and fancy is said to lend color and beauty to the soberest of weekdays.

Read *Gösta Berlings Saga* by Selma Lagerlöf (1858-1940), who was born and grew up in Värmland and later became one of Sweden's foremost authors. (Nobel prize winner in 1909 and later member of the Swedish Academy.) In this book she tells of the blue hills, said to be inhabited by trolls, and makes vivid the picture of beautiful manor houses where gay, carefree people care only for "one long dance of pleasure along the shores of Lake Löven."

From this land of fact and fancy to this country came large groups of people who set out to find a region similar in scenery to their native province where they could feel at home. They never forgot the hillside bordering the lake and how the groves looked at springtime when the yellow flower called *guldviva* covered the ground. They never forgot the deep forest in winter and heavily loaded timber sledges moving slowly over the snowy roads, nor *bruket*, the ironworks, where many were born. Who can tell what a *bruk* is and what makes it memorable? It cannot be translated by the word factory, because it is far more than "a collection of buildings for the manufacture of goods." Rather, it is a whole community, and it is there because of the iron ore deposits and the deep forests all around. It has grown up around an industry and it is usually located in an idyllic setting. Stirring with life and activity, it has all the earmarks of a modern community and still it is a country place. Workers and their families live in attractive cottages and their social life is concentrated on what they can do together, such as practicing an instrument and appearing in concerts, discussing the latest books and maintaining a library, attending lectures by visiting professors, or listening to recitations of poetry read by guest speakers. One could say that a *bruk* is a family concern, in earlier days headed by a patriarch called *brukspatron*, but today managed by a director, usually called *disponent*.

From such a place, called Långbanshyttan, came one of the more well-known men of Värmland, whose imagination and inventive powers came to serve the United States well in time of peril. He was John Ericsson (1803-1889), who spent forty years of his life in this country. As the designer of the iron-clad *Monitor,* which defeated the *Merrimac* in March 1862, he is forever honored in the annals of the United States.

**FREEDOM WITHIN THE LAW**

# FREEDOM WITHIN THE LAW

It would be too staggering a task to try to prove the provinicial loyalty of emigrants from each part of Sweden and to continue to deal with the hereditary principles which came to influence the course of their lives in this country. It seems important, however, to point out the one trait in common that is true of most Swedish-born men and women, regardless of birthplace. That is respect for law and order, and it is deep-rooted, applicable to kings and knaves alike. The sentiment of one Swedish king, Karl XV (1859-1872), is gleaned from his official motto *Land skall med lag byggas* (The nation must be built with law). The present king of Sweden, Gustaf VI Adolf, who celebrated his eighty-eighth birthday on November 11, 1970, has as his personal code *Plikten framför allt* (Duty above all) and lives by it.

Those who are "knaves" have imbibed the same principle of honor, whatever can be said about their living up to it. The rule of law in Sweden is a concept, the people's concept of justice. It goes back through centuries to medieval times and to the province of Västergötland where the first code of rules was conceived and maintained. Through oral tradition the law was known and recognized from generation to generation. One may wonder how. A most important reason was that the language of the codes impressed the people with its robust and vigorous wording.

Furthermore, the codes dealt with the subject at hand directly and without elaboration. In places, the codes were not altogether devoid of a poetic rhythm which also served as a handle for memorization. Briefly and forcefully they stipulated the established rules by which an offender was to be punished, or adjustments made. Here are a few examples from *The Law of the West Goths,* translated by Alfred Bergin:

"A man kills another in church, that is felony, punished by exile or death. A man ties another to a tree in the forest, that is felony.

"Kills someone a Swedish man, or one from Småland, but not from Västergötland, he pays therefore a fine of thirteen marks and eight örtugs and no tribe-fine. Kills someone a Dane or a Norwegian he pays a fine of nine marks.

"One man lends another his slave, he answers for his deed who has received the loan, while he is in his care.

"The housewife shall have power of the chest-keys and incur as well as pay bills.

"Someone dies and his heirs are not found, then the king is his heir. One brother travels as a merchant, and another sits at home in the ashes, both shall inherit alike. The son is the father's heir. If there is no son, the daughter is.

"If any one calls another a bad name, his fine is sixteen silver pieces. If he cuts a man's nose off, he is fined three marks for the offence and nine marks for the wound.

"If a bell falls down from the belfry and is hitting someone on the head and he dies, the parish pays fine for three marks.

"The king wishes to ask for himself a wife. Is it outside the kingdom, then he shall let his men go thither and present his errand and receive pledge. Then the king shall prepare for the bridal trip. The king shall go to meet her and give twelve marks in gold or two villages as security.

"A freeholder's son wishes to ask a wife for himself, he shall visit the nearest relative and begin his asking. He has the right to appoint a betrothal meeting. At this meeting shall the amount of property be agreed upon, land determined, if there is land, and all that they wish to give. Three marks shall be a legal friendgift (a gift by the groom to the marriage spokesman). As soon as the betrothal is performed and the hands have been joined, then all the betrothal presents (gifts to any of the bride's friends) are won, but the friendgift not before they come upon the same mattress and under the same quilt."

Although justice was administered with care there were cases when unreasonable measures were taken. Musicians, "those who go about with a jew's harp, carry a fiddle or drum," were harshly dealt with. "When a player is wounded, then shall they take a wild heifer and bring it up on top of a hill. Then some one shall shave all the hair off the tail and grease it. Then some one shall bring the player a pair of greased shoes. Then he shall take the heifer by the tail and some one shall strike hard with a sharp lash. If he is able to hold, then he shall have that good beast and enjoy it as a dog enjoys grass (that is, not have any good out of it, but do as a dog when he has eaten grass, vomit it up)."

The judicial assembly of the freemen in the region was called *ting,* and the authority and commanding force, *lagman* or lawman. He knew the law well and could recite it by heart. One can visualize the scene as the sturdy, rugged freeholders gathered in a meadow or hillside where rocks furnished seating places for some while the rest of the crowd milled about. As a shield was struck with a crashing blow, there was silence and the voice of the

lawman rang out as he presented the cases to be heard.
No one was punished unheard. Aside from having
authority, it can be assumed that the lawman was a man
of physical strength standing before his "court," a towering
figure holding his listeners rapt and tense by the magic
power of the short, snappy phrases of the law code.

One would like to think that Eskil Magnusson was
such a man, but tall or short, fat or thin, he shall be
remembered forever for having compiled the laws into
one document. About 1200 this work came into being
and is called *Äldre Västgötalagen* (The Elder Law of the
West Goths). The chronicles tell that Eskil was the seventeenth lawman of Västergötland, and that he "meditated
upon the laws with much skill and personal foresight . . .
He was a great man, very gifted, and was above all the
chiefs of the land . . . What more can be said of him than
that late if ever will again be born such a man."

Eskil's brother, the mighty Birger Jarl (died in 1266),
was also a lawmaker. As regent during the infancy of his
son Valdemar, he ruled with a strong hand, establishing
law and order in the kingdom. His laws of peace, called
*fridslagarna,* were to insure security in the home, in church,
and at the *ting,* as well as to guarantee protection to women.
Birger Jarl is also the author of the inheritance law for
women, who before this time could inherit only if no brother
existed.

Later, during the reign of Magnus Eriksson, the laws
from different parts of Sweden were gathered into one
general law, called *landslag.* Established about 1350, it
was finally accepted by all regions at the beginning of the
fifteenth century. It was recodified into the present Swedish
law of 1734.

At the same time as adherence to the law is claimed
as being one of the dominant characteristics of a Swede,

it must hastily be added that he regards freedom within the law as equally consequential. He abides by the laws of the land while moving freely within them. When the powerful bishop Thomas Simonsson of Strängnäs (died in 1443) wrote the pithy lines on freedom, he was agitated and concerned for the freedom of his country. Little did he know that these lines would live on and be quoted throughout the centuries. They reflect an unwavering belief in liberty and justice:

> "Frihet är det bästa ting,
> Som sökas kan all världen kring
> För den henne rätt kan bära.
> Vill du vara dig själver huld,
> Så älska frihet mer än guld,
> Ty frihet följer ära."

Several translations have been made of these lines— this writer offers the following:

> In all the world
> Freedom is the noblest thing to strive for—
> For the one who justly can uphold it.
> If you want to be true to yourself,
> Then love freedom more than gold,
> For with freedom follows honor.

# THE SWEDISH NATIONAL ANTHEM

Du gamla, du fria, du fjällhöga Nord,
Du tysta, du glädjerika sköna!
Jag hälsar dig vänaste land uppå jord,
Din sol, din himmel, dina ängder gröna,
Din sol, din himmel, dina ängder gröna.

Du tronar på minnen från fornstora dar,
Då ärat ditt namn flög över jorden.
Jag vet att du är och du blir vad du var.
Ja, jag vill leva, jag vill dö i Norden!
Ja, jag vill leva, jag vill dö i Norden!

Words by Richard Dybeck (1811-1877)


Thou ancient, thou free, thou mountain-crested North,
Thou still, thou joyful, thou beauteous land!
I greet thee, fairest land on earth,
Thy sun, thy sky, thy meadows green,
Thy sun, thy sky, thy meadows green.

Thou rest on memories from the great days of old,
When honored thy name swept around the world.
I know that thou art and remain what thou were.
Yes, I want to live, I want to die in the North!
Yes, I want to live, I want to die in the North!

THE SWEDISH FLAG

# THE SWEDISH FLAG

The blue and yellow flag of Sweden was already at the time of Gustaf Vasa's reign established as the national symbol. It became firmly accepted after his death in 1560, when the country was forced to maintain its power and show its color at sea. The three-tongued banner remained the emblem of the naval fleet, whereas merchant ships were forbidden to carry the crown emblem and had to change to flags with a straight edge. Taken as trophies by Dutch ships in the battle in Öresund in 1658, two three-tongued flags are now kept in Rijkmuseum in Amsterdam. They are the oldest Swedish flags known to exist today.

It was King Oscar II who in 1873 decreed that the flag should wave at the palace in Stockholm whenever he was residing there, a custom that has been observed by all succeeding kings. By some subjects it was first considered an expression of royal conceit, while initiated persons pointed to Oscar II's predilection for the navy and its traditions accorded the flag, acquired during his service as a young officer in the Royal Swedish Navy. In time the custom of hoisting the flag became established, and today the Swedish flag waves from all official buildings as well as from high flagpoles by the humblest cottage—on lesser occasions as well as on national holidays.

The name day of Gustav, June 6, has become national

flag day. Great crowds of spectators gather at the flag-
bedecked stadium in Stockholm to watch the king distribute the blue and yellow banners to leaders of scout
brigades, *Sveriges Lotta* (The Women's Army Auxiliary
Corps), housewives associations, and other societies. To
the thundering music of a military band the large units
come marching in, carrying their banners high, and lower-
ing them as the royal box is passed. It is an impressive
sight, and when the sun is shining from a blue sky against
which the fluttering flags are silhouetted, it becomes a
spectacle one remembers. *Svenska Flaggans Dag* (The
Swedish Flag Day) in 1962 was such an occasion. Countess
Estelle Bernadotte of Wisborg, the American born wife
of the late Folke Bernadotte, gave the main address. Widely
traveled, she lingered on her observations of the Swedes
she had met in different parts of the world and how they
even after many years abroad still expressed their love for
Sweden and for its symbol, the flag of blue and yellow.

It was around 1790 that Carl Michael Bellman (see
chapter "There Is a Musical Strain" . . .) paid homage
to the Swedish flag in the lines, *Över hjältens blom-
sterkrönta skjul, blåser Nordens flagga blå och gul*
(Above the flower-crowned mound waves the blue and
yellow Nordic flag). The entire poem, entitled *"Flaggan på
Nordians hög"* (The Flag on the Nordian Mound), is re-
printed in *Bellmansstudier 1961* by Olof Byström, well-
known Bellman scholar and author of several books and
articles on Bellmaniana. The occasion was a visit to King
Nordian's burial mound, located in Åshusby in Norrsunda
parish, Uppland, when the Swedish flag had been hoisted
above the mound. In a mood of patriotic fervor Bellman
is supposed to have sung the lines extemporaneously. Dr.
Byström does not think it was that simple. He assumes
the poet had been informed of the occasion when he was

visiting his friend Johan Olofsson Schagerström, on whose estate the mound was located, and that he had worked out the poem on paper beforehand. What is remarkable is that in those days the Swedish flag was used only as an official national emblem, and its appearance on a burial mound was extraordinary. Evidently it was this fact that prompted Bellman to write the poem.

During the union with Norway (1814-1905), a union emblem was inserted in the upper left hand corner of the flags of the two countries. The existing regulations for the national flag of Sweden were laid down by law on June 22, 1906.

The proportions of the flag in length to width shall be 16 to 10, the inner fields being 5 to 4 and the outer fields 9 to 4.

THE GREAT COAT OF ARMS

## THE SWEDISH COAT OF ARMS

# THE SWEDISH COAT OF ARMS

The use of heraldic emblems goes far back in history. They were first used on weapons, on shields and banners, and later to characterize personal possessions. Those who possessed worldly goods were prone to signify ownership by attaching their family bearings, or coat of arms. In the fifteenth and sixteenth centuries the phrase actually meant a garment worn over the armor. It was embellished with the family heraldic emblem, thus being easily recognized as the wearer appeared in battle or knightly sports.

Kingdoms and nations were also recognized by heraldic emblems. The lion and the three crowns have long been Sweden's national symbol, the earliest known date being 1238, when *folkungalejonet* (the Folkung lion) was the recognized emblem of Birger Jarl, regent and member of the renowned Folkung dynasty. As the rule of Magnus Ladulås, Birger's son, began, the emblem was emblazoned with a crown over the head of the lion.

The three crowns have caused scholars many headaches. It is established, though, that King Albrekt of Mecklenburg from the beginning of his reign in 1364 carried the emblem of the three crowns. Later, it was the illustrious nobleman Karl Knutsson Bonde, co-regent with Engelbrekt, who actually established the combined composition of the lion and the three crowns, which ever since has constituted the great seal of Sweden.

So far the scholars agree. They also agree that the three crowns did not represent the union of Denmark, Norway, and Sweden under Queen Margareta, but that the emblem was the national symbol of Sweden only.

The great seal is divided into four parts, creating a cross, and in the center is a smaller emblem, the heart shield, which has always carried the coat of arms of the reigning dynasty. When Gustaf Vasa became king in 1523, he inserted the image of the sheaf, *Vasakärven,* which was his family emblem. This sheaf design remained in the national coat of arms even after the Bernadotte dynasty began to rule in 1818 with Karl XIV Johan as king. As prince of Ponte Corvo, a distinction given to Marshal Bernadotte by Napoleon after the battle at Austerlitz in 1805, the new French possessor of "the curved bridge"—a small Italian dominion—adopted as his coat of arms a turreted bridge of silver topped with an eagle. This emblem, augmented by stars above the eagle, was added to the Vasa sheaf on the great seal when Karl Johan began his reign as king of Sweden.

It was not until in 1908 that the Swedish great seal was made legal, establishing a smaller seal of three crowns as used earlier and a large coat of arms of richer ornamentation. Against a background of white ermine and red velvet, topped by a crown, the two lions are holding up the shield in the latter emblem. This national coat of arms is frequently displayed and often seen on the glass door leading into a store that delivers goods to the royal court. The smaller seal is shown on five-crown bills, for instance, together with *moder Svea,* a female figure personifying Sweden. In later printings she is standing up and looks rather streamlined, whereas the older version portrays a seated woman of imposing stature with a horn of plenty in her arms and the lion at her feet. As the United States is symbolized by Uncle Sam and Britain by John Bull, Sweden is identified by *moder Svea*.

The recent salvaging of the Swedish man-of-war, called *Vasaskeppet,* which sank in Stockholm harbor in 1628, has uncovered a multitude of interesting items from that period. A shield carved in oak bearing the emblem of the three crowns is among the findings displayed in a museum especially built for the Vasa treasures. To anyone whose interests embrace heraldic symbols there is a gratifying field of opportunity for study in Sweden's libraries, museums, and castles.

**RESPECT FOR LEARNING**

# RESPECT FOR LEARNING

It began early. From the first conscious awareness of a book the Swedish child learned the importance of knowledge. And the advantages were tangible from the start. On the cover of the ABC book there was a picture of a rooster and the story was told that through some mysterious powers he would reward any little boy or girl who studied hard and learned the letters quickly with something good to eat, or perhaps even a coin. The saying was *Tuppen värper* which meant that the rooster will lay—as the hen lays eggs—goodies of some sort. It was all very puzzling. How could the rooster know if one studied or not? But he did. After a long session with the book and the *pekpinne* (pointer) it happened. Leaving the book for a while and returning later, the little pupil would find a piece of candy, a chocolate bar, an orange, or an apple tucked in between the pages. *Tuppen har värpt!* And the urge to learn had begun.

To clarify the significance of these bestowals an explanation is in order. In those days when the rooster was a power to reckon with, goodies were not generally available to a Swedish child, that is, except in meager measures. Even in well established households a child's food was rationed to a certain extent, especially cookies and candy. Therefore, it was a treat to get a cookie or a piece of candy. And the taste of an orange or a banana was identified with parties and company. Fruit, imported to a large extent, was costly and when father on rare occasions came home with a colorful paper bag from the flower shop, where fruit was bought, many pairs of eyes followed every move of his hands as they dipped into the fruit and began portioning it out. It was an event.

Cultivated throughout adult life, respect and love for learning run like a red thread through the Swedish make-up. Striving for an education is a common urge and many who have not had the opportunity of more schooling than the obligatory years regard it a great handicap. Such a book-hungry Swede may join a reading circle or attend evening school, or take time off from his job to enter a folk high school. He studies for the sheer enjoyment of learning. Through the years several Swedish poets and writers have begun their literary careers in such a school.

Today public libraries furnish free reading material to communities in all parts of Sweden. Well established correspondence schools offer authorized courses leading to a degree. Among the numerous study circle organizations the ABF is the largest. The letters stand for *Arbetarnas Bildnings-Förbund*—Workers' Educational Association. Literature and languages are popular subjects, but political and economic issues are also studied and discussed.

In Sweden a person of learning is looked up to. Aside from the enrichment of mind, an education brings to the individual added social prestige, and this is particularly true regarding academic degrees. Ambitious parents often try to persuade their offspring to enter schools leading to a university degree. Many sons and daughters have been coerced and wheedled and coaxed to procure the white velvet cap called *studentmössan,* which symbolizes the open way for studies at a university, even though their minds were not geared to book learning. In most cases, however, the choice is voluntary, although long years of intensive study lie ahead. But finally, when the written tests have been passed and the day of oral examination has come out successfully, the relief and joy of that moment make up for the long years of preparation. The day stands as a milestone and is significant in many ways.

While the candidates struggle and sweat before the examining board within the building, parents, relatives, and friends have been waiting outside the college throughout the late afternoon hours, expecting the examination that began in the morning to be over at any time. But there is still a long wait. Throughout the crowd flowers are in evidence. There are small corsages tied with long streamers in blue and yellow and long-stemmed roses or carnations tied with soft bows of raffia. The atmosphere is tense, because everyone present is concerned. All are casting glances at one of the windows in an upper floor from which the signal will be given. Family and friends alike cannot hide the dreadful thought of a possible failure.

Finally the moment comes. In the window there is a wild display of white caps and in the next minute a group of weary but triumphant graduates come storming out of the main entrance. An outburst of cheers and shouts greets them. *Studenten* who up to this moment was a *gymnasist* (undergraduate) has now "arrived" and is at once surrounded by family and friends who congratulate him and pin their roses on his coat or hang the corsages around his neck by a whirl of ribbons, making him look like a flower-bedecked maypole. Strong arms lift him up and toss him in the air while onlookers cheer. *Studentskan,* that is, the girl graduate, is given the same rough treatment. All are gripped with the same feeling of relief and triumph. Only those whose son or daughter failed to make the grade will quietly steal away from the scene.

Young shrill voices are heard striking up the traditional student song as the crowd slowly moves out toward the street. Flower-trimmed vehicles—trucks or open cars—are waiting to bring the newly capped students to their homes. The street will be jammed and the traffic stops. But the officer in charge smiles indulgently. Every onlooker is seized with the carnival spirit. In smaller places the whole community participates in the joyful event.

At home a festive dinner is prepared. As the family and friends are gathered around the table, many toasts are proposed and words of pride and praise are spoken. The student has upheld the honor of the family and is the recipient of more commendation than has ever come his way before.

Later in the evening, as the graduates gather for a celebration of their own, the traditional song about the student's happy day is sung over and over again until voices grow hoarse and husky. The day will indeed be remembered as *studentens lyckliga dag*.

Pitiful is the situation of the undergraduate who fails in the final examination. He is known to have rushed down to the railroad station and there hopped on the first train out, regardless of direction, just to get away from pitying glances. Upon return in a day or two, he may explain that he could not face his family at the dinner which his mother had planned with such love and attention. Due to his failure the day of festivity had turned into one of greatest disappointment, and he was not strong enough to face it. Others may join their family at dinner, trying to make the best of a bad situation. Fortunately, those who fail are not many.

In Sweden today the opportunities for a higher education are open to a far greater number of students than before, and with the recently established *grundskola* (a comprehensive or basic school) the road to get ahead is clearly outlined. Through this new school system every Swedish boy and girl will have a chance for higher learning, if he or she so chooses, without any social or financial discrimination.

Beginning at a stage corresponding to the third college year in the United States, Sweden's four universities, located at Uppsala, Lund, Stockholm, and Göteborg, offer instruction on the highest level in theology, law, medicine, humanities, and natural sciences. The recently established graduate school in Umeå concentrates on medicine and dentistry and the renowned Caroline Institute in Stockholm, as the traditional center for medical studies, attracts students of medicine from countries far and near. It is connected with a large modern hospital.

"Reading maketh a full man," says Sir Francis Bacon (1561-1626), English philosopher, statesman, and author, in one of his essays. "Some books are to be tasted, others to be swallowed, and some few to be chewed and digested. . . ."

A Swede's appetite for books embraces many fields. Whereas in earlier times a modest home would have only the Bible and Luther's *Postilla* in its cupboard—and in some circles also the works of contemporary authors—a modern Swedish home proudly holds attractive book cases with a display of fine books clearly showing signs of being read. They are mostly novels, but books on birds, fish, butterflies, mushrooms, and other nature subjects are also in evidence. Thus the book business flourishes. Over 5,000 titles are published annually, which is a handsome figure for a small country. Books on poetry are sold in comparatively impressive editions. Swedes of today enjoy modern trends in poetry and appraise the new translations of works by foreign writers with keen ears for sound and rhythm. American plays and dramas have especially appreciative audiences in Swedish theatres, as well as avid readers.

With the approach of fall and long dark evenings ahead the interest in reading is enhanced above the usual attention to books, and when by October the new literary works begin to appear in the book store windows, prospective buyers crowd in. They stand in line at the book counters. Book weeks are scheduled when authors generally are available for autographs, and reading circles are formed, offering favorable terms for loans and purchases. This great interest in books is reflected in the Christmas buying. Favorite aunts and uncles, boy friends and girl friends alike, are given books as presents for Christmas. And the book sales are stimulated by the lively advertising and by the impressive space given to literary criticism and book reviews in the daily press. While this is a regular feature of the leading newspapers in Sweden during the twelve months of the year, it is increased in the months before Christmas. The titles of new books meet the eye everywhere and make an imprint.

**GOING TO CHURCH**

# GOING TO CHURCH

Much has been said from this side of the world about the empty churches in Sweden. And it is true that church attendance is irregular compared with attendance in American churches. On holidays, however, most Swedish churches are filled to the door. To attend the early service on Christmas Day, called *julotta,* is a must with most Swedes, and on Easter Sunday the attendance is equally active. Churchgoers are just as faithful during Advent. It is in the summer time when tourists visit Sweden that the churches show up their emptiness. As is mentioned elsewhere in this book, the urge to spend the summer months out-of-doors on every free Sunday supersedes the inclination to go to church. A Swede actually feels it is his duty to his children, as well as to himself and to his wife, to take advantage of the sun and air and the beautiful countryside in gaining a healthy tan, relaxation, and rest.

In earlier times attending church services on Sundays was far more a matter of tradition than it is today. Country women often wore a black shiny silk *schalett*—a fringed head cloth or kerchief—which during the weekdays was kept nicely folded in a bureau drawer. When going to church, it was customary to have a little sprig of salvia or lavender in the fold of the handkerchief and to lift it to the nose from time to time when the preaching was apt to lull the listeners into drowsiness. Women of means kept the herbs in a small silver case, which they carried under the hymnbook.

Going to church also meant meeting relatives and friends. This was especially true among country people who lived far from each other. They would nod at their kinsfolk as they sat in church, the women to the left of the main aisle and the men to the right, and after the service they would stop outside and gather into groups for a chat. There many sundry matters were discussed and ironed out before leaving for home.

Very few of the parishioners had had a chance to talk with the minister. He did not stand by the door shaking hands with them as they walked out. It was not the custom in those days. In official matters when they called at his office—*pastorsexpeditionen*—they would of course see him, or his assistant pastor, and at parish meetings. But socially, especially during holidays, when great feasting took place on the farms in the region, the parishioners came closer to their *präst* than at any other time, because he was the honored guest and most likely inclined to speak to every one present. Some of these old clergymen were colorful individuals who on weekdays displayed the same weaknesses as most people, but on Sundays turned into an awe-inspiring figure in clerical robes, preaching a sermon of fire and damnation from the pulpit. Seldom has a *prost* of this order been more vividly portrayed than in the poem *"Våran prost,"* written from the parishioner's point of view by the great Värmland poet Gustaf Fröding (1860-1911):

> Våran prost
> är rund som en ost
> och lärd som själva den onde,
> men gemen likväl
> och en vänlig själ

och skäms ej, att far hans var bonde.
Han lever som vi
och dricker sitt kaffe med halva i
som vi
och ratar icke buteljen,
älskar mat
som vi
och är lat
som vi
—men annat är det vid helgen.

Så fort han fått prästrocken på,
vi andra känna oss ynkligt små,
men prosten likasom växer,
för då är han prost från topp till tå
och det en hejdundrande prost ändå
i stort pastorat med annexer.
Jag glömmer väl aldrig i all min dar,
hur vördig han var
här om sistens i kappan och kragen,
hur världens barn
han malde i kvarn
och läste för köttet lagen!
Och prosten grät
—tacka för det,
han talte om yttersta dagen!

Och alla gräto vi ymnigt med,
ty köttet sved
och själen var allt satt i klämma.
Och kyrkrådet smög sig med ryggen i kut
vid tjänstens slut
efter prosten ut,
ty kyrkrådet var kallat till stämma.

Men det förstås,
vi repade oss,
när prosten klarade strupen
till sist och sade: "Välkomna
till smörgåsbordet och supen!"

"To translate poetry into prose, no matter how faithfully and even subtly the words are reproduced, is to betray
a poem."

So says the American poet Edna St. Vincent Millay.
Feeling the weight of that statement, as well as the truth
of it, I must nevertheless attempt to render a line by line
translation, although my words cannot possibly give as
vivid a picture of the imposing *prost* as he appears in the
original, nor catch the basic rhythm of the lines. For those
readers who have to resort to the translation the loss is
great. How much more rewarding to read and rejoice
over the poem as written! If for no other reason, learning
Swedish would be worth the effort. Only by reading the
poem as written can you visualize the large, rotund figure
likened unto a cheese. The poet, knowing his countrymen,
perhaps used this simile because it was familiar and con-
veniently near to the farming people, who usually had their
store houses filled with big and shiny home-made cheeses,
which had to have regular care. They must be turned and
washed and wiped and looked over for fear bulges might
develop. The farmers regarded their cheese "crop" as an
investment in good living. It was close to their hearts. To
liken the girth of their own worthy *prost* to a cheese was
complimentary. They liked him to be one with them, they
liked him to enjoy his eats and drinks as they did, but they
also liked him to take his ministerial offices seriously. They
respected him for his book learning, for his great dignity
and awesome aplomb as he appeared before them in

church. Will he come out like that in English dress?

> Our Dean
> is round as a cheese
> and learned as the devil himself,
> but sociable anyway
> and a kind soul
> and is not ashamed that his father was a farmer.
> He lives like we do
> and "spikes" his coffee
> as we do
> and does not reject the bottle,
> loves food
> as we do
> —but on holidays, that's something else.
>
> As soon as he dons the clerical robe
> the rest of us feel miserably small,
> but the Dean seems to grow
> because then he is Dean from top to toe
> and a magnificent Dean at that
> in a large parish with accessions.
> I shall never forget in all my days,
> how imposing he was
> recently, in his robe and his collar,
> how he put the worldly humans
> through the mill
> and laid down the law to us!
> And the Dean wept,
> no wonder,
> he spoke of the Judgment Day!
>
> And all of us wept profusely, too,
> because it stung the flesh

and the soul was under pressure.
And the church council members sneaked out
with stooped backs
behind the Dean
because they were called to a meeting.
But of course
we recovered
when the Dean finally cleared his throat
and said: "Welcome
to the *smörgåsbord* and the schnapps!"

Every Swede is by birth a member of the Lutheran
State Church and he remains a member unless he with-
draws by formal notification. Today there is complete
religious freedom in Sweden and nearly half a million
Swedes worship in other churches than the State Church.
However, only about 0.5 per cent of the population have
formally had their names removed from the records and
more than 90 per cent of the Swedes are baptized and
married within the State Church. Because of the meticulous
care with which the civic office of the church keeps records
and statistics, grandchildren of Swedish immigrants can
by consulting the parish books learn the date of birth,
baptism, marriage, and emigration of their ancestors.

The largest independent denominations are the Mission
Covenant, the Pentecostal Movement, the Salvation Army,
the National Evangelical Society, the Baptists, and the
Methodist Church. The Roman Catholics, to a great extent
post-war refugee immigrants, number about 28,000, and
there are nearly 15,000 members of the Jewish faith in
Sweden today. The religious radio services, presented by
nonconformist groups as well as State Church represent-
atives, attract a multitude of listeners.

The American Congregation in Stockholm, recently

established, embraces all faiths and bases its services on the ecumenical principle.

Sweden is divided into thirteen dioceses or *stift,* each headed by a bishop. The archbishop resides in Uppsala. On special occasions he preaches in the time-honored cathedral robed in full canonicals. At an ordinary service an officiating Swedish clergyman wears either a vestment or a long, black pleated cape over his black frock coat.

In recent years a controversy within the State Church has stirred up heated arguments pro and con. Should a woman minister be accepted? In 1957 the Swedish *Riksdag* (Parliament) passed a law permitting women in the pulpit. A few years elapsed, however, before the State Church accepted it. A group of Swedish clergymen, assembled under the name *Kyrklig samling* or Church Union, keeps insisting that a woman minister has no place in the church. The former bishop Bo Gierts has been the leading force in the opposition.

Under great difficulties many Swedish women have succeeded in completing their studies for the ministry, and at present (1970) there are more than thirty women of the cloth in the Swedish State Church. Their influence on parish life is said to be most beneficial. It has proven that in things like counseling and dealing with marital problems a woman minister has the edge on her male colleagues. It is the consensus that some men find it easier to confide in a woman than in a man.

In earlier times the churchgoing public had become discontent with the impersonal sermons and with the aloof manner of the clergy. The cold and formal services left the heart untouched. Furthermore, up until about 1860 denominations other than Lutheran were forbidden and even private religious meetings without a Lutheran pastor were prohibited. It was at this point that stories of America,

the land of religious freedom, began to stir the imagination.
A mass emigration was set in motion. This phase of Swedish
history is exhaustively treated in *The Religious Aspects of
Swedish Immigration* by the late George M. Stephenson,
professor of history, University of Minnesota.

# WEDDING AND BRIDAL CUSTOMS

# WEDDING AND BRIDAL CUSTOMS

In Sweden today one can get married without *lysning,* that is without the publication of banns which was a must earlier. And it seems that couples planning to marry are welcoming the new law which took effect on July 1, 1969, thereby dismissing the old ceremony. But before a marriage can take place it must be determined whether there is any impediment to the matrimonial union. This procedure, called *hindersprövning,* is handled by the pastor of the parish where the bride-to-be is registered, or in the parish where she lives. It is advised that the applicants contact the officiating pastor well in advance for information of what other documents, if any, are required. It should be pointed out that the applicants must appear in person. An affidavit stating that the persons in question are free from earlier marriage bonds is usually considered sufficient, but it has to be signed by two people who know the applicants well. It is advised to have the document notarized. Compared with the earlier law when *lysning* was obligatory before a marriage could take place, it is now a simple matter to get official sanction. The marriage ceremony can be performed at civil court or in the church. Should a couple want the reading of the banns at a Sunday service, it is done just once instead of three Sundays in succession as it was done before.

The wedding can be an elaborate church wedding or a simple ceremony at the courthouse. Wearing a crown and veil is a custom steeped in tradition. In no other land has the church played such a prominent role in maintaining and preserving the tradition of the bridal crown as in Sweden. This festive symbol of a marriage ceremony has for generations been cherished with respect, and if a young girl forfeited her right to wear it, she was subjected to derision. An interesting transmutation of the idea of right and wrong in wearing a crown is revealed in a Dala peasant painting (Jufwas Anders Ersson, 1802) which depicts the five wise and the five foolish virgins. The latter do wear crowns, but these are placed askew, whereas the crowns on the five wise virgins are worn straight.

In the fourth part of his emigrant chronicle, Vilhelm Moberg gives an interesting narrative of a bridal crown. Ulrika from Västergöhl, a fascinating character, defiant of law and order, who in her youth was shut out from communion with her church in Ljuder because of her unchaste way of life, had emigrated to America and in later years settled down as Mrs. Henry O. Jackson, well established wife of a minister in Minnesota. She found a unique way of "revenge" on her former parishioners. Anonymously she made a donation to Ljuder church in the form of a silver bridal crown, set with precious stones. There was a stipulation. It could only be worn by those known to be chaste and honorable. Ulrika's life-long dream of being accepted would be fulfilled, she meant, each time a young woman from Ljuder parish wore the silver crown with the precious stones.

Among the first known adornments for the head of a young unmarried woman was *piglocken,* a stuffed headband wrapped with colorful ribbons which continued in streamers down the back. It was also called *huvudla* or shortened to *hlad-la.* Later these headgears became more elaborate and were finally shaped into the traditional bridal crown of today, executed in silver and gold and often enhanced with precious stones. But to the intervening generations only a myrtle crown would do. It is a crown-shaped wireframe wound with sprigs of myrtle—a shrub-like plant with ovate evergreen leaves, sacred to Venus, according to the ancients. On most of the old wedding pictures the bride wears the traditional myrtle and a long veil. The dress is often white, but in many cases black. The bride holds in her hand a small, tightly trimmed bouquet with long ribbons. If standing alone, she often rests her hand on a gate of unpeeled birch, evidently to steady herself for the ordeal. Photography was not done by snap methods in those days! Looking through the family album we also find the sitting bride, while the bridegroom stands stiffly at her side with hands looking awkward in white gloves.

Many a modern Swedish woman cherishes the traditional myrtle crown as did her mother and grandmother before her. Some years ago when a young woman arrived from Sweden to marry an official of the Swedish consulate in Minneapolis, the wedding was almost cancelled because of the lack of myrtle. Finally, a radio appeal was made and a discerning woman from Saint Paul came to the rescue offering her plant. The crown was made and the bride beamed! On a later occasion, when anticipating such a dilemma, another Swedish bride-to-be had her crown flown directly from Sweden.

Selma Lagerlöf, Sweden's storyteller par excellence, tells in her childhood recollections, *Mårbacka,* about what happened to her maiden aunt Lovisa, who, being asked to trim a myrtle crown for a woman in the parish, deceitfully added lingonberry leaves to augment the scanty supply of myrtle. For this act of deception Lovisa Lagerlöf suffered great pangs of conscience, and when her own engagement to a widowed clergyman with four children was broken, she blamed it on her deceitfulness. One does not substitute lingonberry leaves for myrtle without paying the penalty, she sighed.

How about the groom? Although not as brilliant under
the spotlight as the bride, he is nevertheless a figure to
behold in his conventionally elegant *frack* (white tie and
tails) which handsomely sets off the snowmaidenly white-
ness of the bridal gown. It is customary to wear this formal
dress suit at official festivities as well, and at private dinners
when there is some special occasion.

In Dalarna, where the custom of wearing the native
costume has lingered longer than in any other province in
Sweden, a bride and her attendants will often appear in
their parish dress, and the event of her wedding becomes
an eagerly sought tourist attraction. When traveling in
Dalarna one can determine how many farms have had a
wedding recently, because by the gate there would be two
peeled tree trunks on which the top branches have been
left. In other parts of Sweden friends and neighbors usually
erect a leafy archway called *äreport* at the home of the
bride, or outside the place where the bridal couple will
establish their home.

Weddings, with or without ceremonial traditions, are
occasions of dignity, some tears, perhaps, music, and the
shower of rice. In Sweden, after the marriage ceremony,
the bridal party proceeds to a restaurant, if the home is
not large enough to hold those invited. Swedish churches,
at least not the State Churches, have no facilities for re-
freshments as is the case in the United States. At the dinner
the bride and groom are honored with toasts and speeches.
Absent friends generally send telegrams, sometimes very
witty ones, and the official host reads them during the
course of the evening. Music is provided and as the bridal
couple dance the first round, the guests gradually join them
and dancing continues until the wee hours.

In years past weddings in the country were celebrated
for several days, and when a wealthy farmer married off

his daughter the whole parish knew of it. When relatives and friends came from a distance they stayed overnight. Older guests occupied all available sleeping quarters while young people slept in their clothes on the floor, so-called *syskonbädd*, meaning a brother-and-sister bed.

The preparation of food for such large groups of people began weeks before the event and busy hands slaughtered and cooked and baked and brewed. One wonders how the father of the bride could stand the cost of such a spread, but no doubt the prestige it rendered made up for it. To accommodate the guests at mealtime an outdoor dining space was provided by setting up a tent or making a shelter of boughs and branches in which long tables and benches were placed. Most of the time the guests were occupied with eating, but often there were intervals of dancing between the courses. The nearby barn would provide a sturdy dance floor and before the wedding celebration was over all the male guests would try to *dansa kronan av bruden,* that is, dance with the bride so unrestrainedly that the crown would fall off her head. According to tradition, the man who caught it would be the next one to marry. The music was furnished by fiddlers in the parish neighborhood, who often competed in fanciful playing, or by a farm-hand pumping his accordion.

On the morning of the second day the bride appeared in black, signifying her status as a married woman. Contrary to the day before, when she sat quietly in her white finery, she could from now on assist her mother in tending to the needs of the guests. Not until all the people in the parish had been entertained, even to the inmates in the poorhouse, could she and her husband begin to pack her chest of linens and multitude of wedding presents in the buggy and start for their new home. In her chest would be dozens and dozens of sheets and pillowcases with

fluted tie-ribbons, tablecloths from the large banquet size
to smaller ones for different size tables, and stacks of
napkins, all in shiny, smooth linen and marked with her
initials. Most often the linens were her own handiwork, as
weaving and sewing constituted an accepted part of a
young woman's training. Today, a Swedish bride is more
likely to have a linen shop furnish her needs, although
weaving is still a favorite avocation in Sweden.

For a bride and groom without means, or who do not
care to use available funds for a wedding feast, a marriage
ceremony may be held privately in church, or before the
magistrar at the courthouse. Only 6 per cent of Swedish
women choose the latter, however. Incidentally, the legal
marriageable age is eighteen for a woman and twenty-one
for a man.

In Sweden the American custom of giving a "shower"
would be a novelty. But the one pre-wedding festivity that
a bride-to-be can expect is a *möhippa*. The word *mö* means
maiden and *hippa* a party of unceremonious character.
Having been assured that she has no engagement for a
certain evening, her girl friends actually kidnap her. Watching at her office entrance, or place of work, they throw
a sack or cloth over her head as she steps out and turn
her around several times to confuse her as to the direction
of the jaunt. With laughter and jolly banter, they bring
her to the designated place where the other guests are
waiting and where the merrymaking continues throughout
the evening.

For the bridegroom a *svensexa* is in store, arranged
by his male friends. The word *sexa* means a meal eaten
together with likeminded friends. In combinations, the
word takes on a slanted meaning, as in *huggsexa,* a meal
eaten hurriedly, and *sillsexa* when the food is mainly
herring in all forms, and finally *svensexa,* a festive meal

with drinks in honor of a *sven* or bachelor about to marry.

Upon her engagement, that is, when it is officially announced in the papers, a Swedish girl receives from her fiance a plain gold ring, and she gives him the same type of a ring. Both are inscribed inside with their names and the date of the occasion. At the marriage ceremony the bride receives a second gold ring exactly like the first one, the two of which she will wear together throughout the marriage. For the groom there is only one ring. Later on a Swedish wife may be given a diamond ring by her husband —at the birth of her firstborn, perhaps, or on an important birthday. Of course, all birthdays are important in Sweden, but the thirtieth and each decade thereafter carry more weight. Or she may never own a diamond ring. She may prefer a ruby or an emerald!

WHEN DEATH COMES . . .

# WHEN DEATH COMES

In Sweden death is regarded with deep respect and fraught with agelong customs. Mourners follow traditional practices and are resolved that the funeral will be executed with dignity and care. The custom of sending out black-edged invitations to relatives and friends seems to be less observed today. A black-bordered announcement in the papers is the rule. Usually six or seven days elapse between the time of death and the funeral.

The traditional funeral dress for men is *frack,* that is, white tie and full dress suit. The black-frocked women wear hats with heavy veiling over the face, and hose, shoes, gloves, and purse in black. No jewelry is worn, except black beads. This black attire is worn for quite some time after the funeral—formerly a full year—by a woman mourning her father or mother, or husband, or any other close relative. Today the mourning period is much shorter. An elegant touch to a mourning frock is the pointed double collar in crisp white. Even though Swedish women in general dress quite soberly, those in mourning do stand out in a crowd. Foreign visitors in Sweden have expressed amazement at the frequent appearance of black-robed women in the street. After the funeral, a man usually wears a dark suit with a black ribbon across the lapel. Earlier, it was customary to wear a wide black band around the left sleeve.

When death occurs in the country, it is often the custom
to keep the body at home until funeral time. White sheets
are hung before the windows and the walk out to the road
is strewn with finely cut spruce twigs. In the city the
funeral arrangements are usually turned over to an under-
taker.

With bereavement come tears and heartache, and the
Swedish mourner surrenders to his grief. No consolation,
no uplifting thought or word seem to have a place at a
funeral. At the grave the immediate relatives walk up to
the edge and express words of love and affection. Clutched
in their hands are small tributes of flowers which they let
drop into the open grave as a last farewell. Larger bouquets
and wreaths are placed as a frame around the edge, later
to be arranged over the mound. The traditional funeral
hymn, *Jag går mot döden var jag går* (I get nearer death
wherever I go), does not ease the mind of the mourner,
and when the coffin is being lowered and the three scoops
of earth fall with heavy thuds on the lid, all hope seems
drained from his heart.

Many a Swedish poet has had a curious concern for
death. Verner von Heidenstam tells in his memoirs about
the role death played in his childhood games. He buried
his dolls in the ground and at times he himself would
stretch out on the cold ground in the vault of the parish
church to get the feeling of what death was like. Once
when a candle was blown out by a draft from the window,
his father said: "There—a life came to an end." This impressed the young son greatly and for a long time afterwards he had the feeling of taking someone's life whenever
he blew out a candle. One motto he never tired of repeating
was: "One must never forget to visit the graves of relatives." With his beloved *mormor* (grandmother) he frequently visited the cemetery by the little country church,

and when she at times wanted to ride by without stopping, he prompted her to think of the day when she would lie in her grave longing for his visits. How would she feel if he would ride by with the shiny horses and not even get out of the carriage? She always yielded.

It is said that a great help in overcoming grief is to keep hands and heart occupied. And for mourners there are many things they must concern themselves with after the funeral is over. Food is forever a great item in Sweden, be it wedding or funeral, and in earlier times there was feasting of some proportions. The name *gravöl*, as the funeral feast was called, indicates that *öl* or ale was part of it, and stronger drinks, too. Slowly the heavy, somber atmosphere would give way to a more lighthearted mood and often the feasting continued until the next day, or even longer. It was customary that guests brought *förning*, that is, prepared dishes for the table, which naturally was a great help for the bereaved family whose task it was to feed all those gathered in the home. Today, customs are simplified and the funeral may conclude with a dinner at a restaurant. In the country, however, where relatives and friends have come from a distance, there is much feasting before guests depart.

Traditions are deep-rooted. Reflecting on the Swedes' devotion to the memory of a deceased kinsman or friend brings to mind the famous lines from *Havamal,* the great Eddic poem from the Viking times: "Cattle die, kinsmen die, and so will you; but one thing that never dies is the good name of a dead man." This holds true today as of old. The modern Swede is not prone to forget the good name of a deceased relative or friend. The grave is painstakingly cared for and decorated with potted plants or fresh flowers throughout the spring and summer seasons. Neither is the devotion to a memory apt to be forgotten in the daily family life, at least not in homes where traditions play a role. The photograph of the deceased person standing on the mantel or the piano is "remembered" at all times. A vase with fresh flowers always appears at its side. It may be one rose or a carnation, or perhaps a small bouquet of wild flowers when in season. The vase is never without a floral tribute.

A visiting American in Sweden may show his respect for this tradition by furnishing flowers for the home where he is staying, and for the graves of those who have passed away—perhaps mutual relatives. Such a thoughtful gesture will be appreciated.

A SWEDE IS A SWEDE IS A . . .

# A SWEDE IS A SWEDE IS A SWEDE . . .

In an evaluation of a national group and taking a perspective view of its achievements, it is not easy to arrive at the essential core. But in the Swedes there seems to be a quality common to all, namely the effort to achieve the very best, and this comes to light and shines through every accomplishment, be it the making of a wooden spoon or building a house. There is an ingrained urge to do first rate work. Bungling or compromising are not tolerated, and the rule an apprentice learns from the outset is *inget fusk* (no cheating). This thoroughness is reflected in the smallest job. When a housewife asks her husband to fasten a hook, he brings the whole tool chest. "And I could have fixed it with a hairpin," she sighs. Not until top quality work has been achieved does a Swedish man consider himself master of his trade or profession. And this idea makes for constant striving.

Could the American-born epithet, "the dumb Swede," have anything to do with the concept of perfection that every Swedish emigrant carried with him to the new country? In looking for a job, did he stubbornly hold to his standard of craftsmanship, refusing to do anything he knew would be beyond his ability? There are many tales of the first hard years and how men far less fitted to do the job grabbed it on the spot. And such is the way of the world that a person who does not speak up for himself or claim a skill he possesses usually is considered foolish, yes, "dumb." Could it be that his laconic answers, his lack of ready banter, even after he had learned the language reasonably well, coined the phrase? There are those who maintain that fellow workers in camps and workshops initiated the expression, "the dumb Swede." Whatever the cause, the steadfast, silent Swede suffered under it, and many descendants have tales to tell of the resentment it fostered.

In Sweden today thoroughness continues to be the earmark of production, and it is a well-known fact that high quality steel and pulp and paper products find markets all over the world. The S-seal—where quality is tradition— has become the symbol of the Swedish image abroad. And Sweden prospers, bringing a high standard of living for all. Behind the highly developed industrialization is the effort of the individual, still striving for perfection. That he continues to be dissatisfied with many things in his daily life and complains of *Krångel-Sverige,* i.e., the slow procedure of officialdom called red tape, and high taxes, seem to be part of the system.

Generally speaking, within his own unit a Swede feels comfortable and at ease, however, accepts his code of living, and acts uniformly contented. Conformity is a shield behind which a Swede hides his true feelings. A foreign visitor often gets the impression that Swedes are stiff and formal and that it is difficult to penetrate the shell. Attending a gathering, he finds the Swedes uniformly polite, but distant. He does not realize that it is a facade hiding a goodly portion of self-conscious uneasiness. A Swede needs time to get acquainted. Behind the appearance of reserve there is warmth and good will. "But how does one get to it?" the visitor asks. Abrupt jolliness and a slap on the shoulder will not do the trick. It is rather a process of slow melting. An evening at the dinner table with generous amounts of food and drink generally results in a letting down of the barriers. A Swede must be sure. Money does not play a large role in this evaluation process. It is rather a probing whether the visitor is on an equal cultural level or moves in the same circle of friends. That is why a letter of recommendation does much to establish contacts. Receiving an invitation to a Swedish home is a mark of approval and acceptance. And after the reserve is completely broken down, the visitor learns that he will never have a truer, more sincere friend than the Swede.

Having accepted an invitation, it is wise to observe the rules. Punctuality is a must, as there is not often any margin for cocktails. If the dinner invitation is for seven o'clock, you press the button to the host's apartment at precisely seven and in a few minutes you will be seated at the table. If a taxi brought you to the door ahead of time, you wait downstairs. Perhaps other guests have gathered there before you, and not until the cathedral clock in the neighborhood strikes seven do you proceed. If it is the first visit, you bring flowers to the hostess—and remove the tissue paper if possible before handing them over. What one does with the wrapping paper in a crowded *tambur* or hall remains a puzzle even to Swedes well versed in social decorum. One solution is to send the flowers earlier in the day, and the hostess will appreciate your foresightedness.

What has been said here about the aloofness of the Swedes does not in any way hold true when you come to visit relatives. They will receive you warmly, feed you until you beg for respite, and shower you with attention every hour of your stay. In fact, they will fight about you! If coffee in bed does not appeal to you, it is wise to announce it the first evening; otherwise, you will be awakened with a flower-trimmed coffee tray the next morning.

Having established that the Swedes in general are reserved, it must be pointed out here that the trend of democracy is working a great adjustment in Sweden's social life. The class distinction is gradually being leveled off and the association between different social groups is made possible as never before. This contributes to a more communicable way of life and helps to banish awkward self-consciousness. The Swedes themselves joke about it and claim that there is no longer any need for an American to break the ice in a crowded train coach. However, one does encounter situations that demonstrate the opposite. And when a particular case is brought out in the daily column of a Swedish newspaper, one begins to wonder when the wall will crumble—completely.

On a train between Göteborg and Malmö four Swedish men, all strangers to one another, happened to be seated at the same table in the dining car. For fifteen minutes they sat in silence waiting to give their orders, looking out on the swiftly changing scene and stealing a glance now and then at each other. But no one uttered a word. One of the men seemed embarrassed, however. Finally, he could not contain himself any longer. Looking out on the houses and stretches of farmland rushing by, he said:

"It goes fast, doesn't it?"

It was nothing clever, just a hand reaching out. But none of the others made a move—not a word was spoken. At long last the waiter appeared. Another long wait before the food was served. And still the four men sat there in silence. The "talker" wriggled, turned about, looked uneasy.

"But this is fantastic," he blurted out. "Here we are four of us at the same table and no one says a word! It can only happen in Sweden. The minute you travel south

—yes, as soon as you reach Denmark, it would be unthinkable. I traveled by bus in Belgium at one time and all the passengers were as one family. Fruit, sandwiches, wine were offered from all sides and we sang and talked and laughed. By the way, some one told a story about a barber on a train. Have you gentlemen heard it?"

The "talker" looked at his companions eagerly. Their faces were like hewn in stone. They busied themselves with knife and fork, and looked out through the window. Once more the talkative man made an attempt: "Have you gentlemen heard the story?"

The silence grew thicker. Finally one of them said: "Yes."

The air went out of the balloon. Hurriedly the deflated man finished his meal and left.

Is the story exaggerated? Some Swedes would say that it is; others would admit that it is fairly true to form. And the foreign visitor continues his observations and finds that the pattern of conformity is reflected in other ways than that of behavior. Just look at the sameness of appearance, he says. One never knows who is who because the employee is as smartly dressed as his employer, both exhibiting a uniformly high quality in the clothes they wear. *Är det äkta?*—meaning genuinely high grade—is a question of paramount importance to a purchasing Swede. He pinches the fabric, he looks at it through the light, he feels of the thickness in his effort to determine if it is all wool or all linen or true silk before he buys. It may be true that every Swedish woman has "that gray suit" in her wardrobe and that a shopping crowd of women gives an impression of sameness, but it is also true that the gray suit has distinctive features. It is often tailor-made and always of a high quality material. And in this connection one word about the male attire. A Swedish man is equally soberly dressed

—until a visiting American relative or friend persuades him to wear the gay, loud shirt, or the flowery tie brought as gifts. He does it to please, but feels uneasy.

Again, conformity and compliance to rule form the pattern of behavior for a Swede. He is law-abiding and often knows what the national code of legal procedures involves. The book of codified law, *Sveriges Rikes Lag,* authorized in 1734, is known to the majority of Swedes. That is perhaps the reason why there is not as great a demand for lawyers in Sweden as there is in the United States. A Swede will fight for a principle and his rights to the utmost, but on the other hand he will trust his fellow man until convinced to the contrary. Often a handshake is all that is needed to close a business deal, and it is as binding as a signed contract. When Ingemar Johansson, former world heavyweight champion, became involved in a dispute with an American fight promoter about his earnings, he showed a face of utter disbelief and exclaimed: "But we shook hands on it, don't you remember?" Since then he has learned that a handshake does not always spell integrity. Who does not remember from childhood how mother demanded a handshake following one's promise? And if there was any sneaking doubt in one's mind that the promise could not be kept, the outstretched hand was not touched.

Child-rearing in Sweden in former days followed firm rules. And among the first Swedish settlers in America the practice was carried on. It was customary to use the rod, and the wood shed was the place as it had been in "the old country." But perhaps more cruel, or far more lasting in effect, was the established way of treating children in general. It was common that their feelings and budding aspirations were disregarded, or treated with aloof indifference. Many Americans of Swedish descent speak of their frustrations in childhood: "I cannot remember that my father or mother at any time made any visible display of affection for me, and sometimes I ached inside for a little love," they say. And the frustrations of an earlier generation were reflected in the next. But it was not only the want of expressed love that made the childhood pinched and meager. It was the deliberate thwarting of all efforts for self-expression, the deliberate holding down of tendencies to excel. The writer can remember very well her eagerness to show a good report card and how father would look sternly and say: "You can do much better!"

As I grew up the allure of the mirror made me sneak a glance now and then, only to be reprimanded by mother. To look in the mirror was forbidden! *Du ser ingenting ut!* was mother's stern comment as she pushed me away from the looking glass. To be told over and over again that one's looks equal nothing would, and did, subdue any attempt to enhance one's negligible features. But how I did hanker for a gay ribbon in my long braid! In mature years when I asked my mother what her idea was, she said: "I was so afraid that my girls were being vain, so I felt I had to squelch any tendencies in that direction." But childhood frustrations have a way of showing up and often find some way of expression later on. Mine is a silk ribbon tucked in my hair!

Being taught from childhood to observe the rule of modesty, yes, self-effacement, a Swede is deprived of initiative and confidence from the start. And this lack has made its mark on most Swedes of earlier generations. It can be traced to Americans of Swedish descent up to this time. They well know the phrase, *det är ingenting,* which reflects the concept that praise must be minimized. However lovely she thinks her dress is, a Swedish woman of an earlier vintage would invariably reply to a compliment: *"Åh, den här gamla trasan!"* (Oh, this old rag), or something equally disparaging. It would not be modest to accept honest praise by saying "thank you!" Today, the tendency is to ignore the inherent impulse and accept compliments with thanks, but it does not come spontaneously.

In her childhood recollections from Småland, entitled *Livets och årets festdagar* (Life's Festive Days and Annual Celebrations), Elisabeth Bergstrand-Poulsen tells of a summer day when she and her friend Nanny played together outside her home. Her mother came out with plates brimming with strawberries for them, and the two playmates settled in the shade enjoying the treat. As soon as the mother was out of sight Nanny exclaimed:

"Your mother is the most beautiful person in the whole world!"

In her own heart the writer agreed fully, but being the modestly well-mannered little girl she was, she replied:

"My mother? No, she is the homeliest person there ever was! It is your mother who is the most beautiful person in the world."

This noble controversy continued for a while. Each of the little playmates were convinced that it was a mark of virtue to be wrong.

A Swedish professor who had devoted much time to the study of the national characteristics of his countrymen was asked on one occasion to name what he considered the three fundamental traits of the Swedes. He weighed the matter a moment before he replied: *"Jaa—de är innerliga för det första, de älskar naturen för det andra, och— förresten är de ganska hyggliga."*

At first one may argue the point of the designation *innerliga,* considering its meaning as tender or warmly earnest, which the outwardly reserved Swede does not seem to display. On the other hand, the word also connotes sincerity, an innermost heartfelt feeling which surely is a part of a Swede's make-up.

His love of nature is an acknowledged characteristic and in clear evidence as he takes his walks in the woods and enjoys all the growing things around him. A daily walk seems to be one of life's necessities in Sweden. On Sundays family groups stroll out to favorite spots of interest, although the use of motor cars is steadily changing the traditional pattern of living. But some walking is still a must. To the astonishment of a Swedish couple who spent the winter in California, they found very few pedestrians on the city streets. Sometimes they were the only ones strolling down the boulevard. A Swedish woman visiting in Minneapolis recently became irritated at the physical inactivity caused by all the well-meaning people offering her a ride wherever she wanted to go. Finally, at a gathering of relatives she voiced her ultimatum. She would stay for the scheduled time only if given the chance to walk each day. "You Americans are going to lose the use of your legs," she added determinedly. She stayed—and walked.

A Swedish youth who studied at the University of Minnesota a few years ago became interested in a popular girl on the campus and decided to gain her attention. It was only natural that he, when calling her, asked her out for a walk. As he told it later, there was dead silence on the other end of the line. Finally the devastating word came. "Why?" He was furious. "Can you imagine a girl asking a fellow why he wants to take her walking!" Not until he was made aware that the rebuff was reciprocal— that to a popular American girl a date without a car is almost unthinkable—did his indignation subside. The blow that this girl dealt him was enough to avert further romancing.

Fresh air is essential to well-being, says the Swede. He often sleeps with windows open, even in winter. The open-air restaurants and sidewalk cafes that blossom forth in the spring express this inborn craving for the out-of-doors. Each dwelling unit in apartment buildings has a balcony where the baby sleeps in all kinds of weather, and where the mother spends her leisure time knitting and drinking her afternoon coffee. As soon as school is out in June the family packs up and leaves for some favorite spot in *skärgården* (the archipelago along the coasts, especially the aggregation of islands outside Stockholm), or by a lake somewhere, or at a fishing village on the west coast. When the family owns a cottage, they return there year after year. Aside from the four weeks vacation officially granted any job-holder, the father often spends only weekends with his family, but exults in the sun and air so much more on those occasions. To row, or sail, or race across the water in a motor boat are favorite pastimes.

Flowers are also considered one of life's necessities. The housewife does not fail to include a few blossoms among her purchases when marketing. And flowers can be had wherever she turns. Aside from the frequent flower shops, there are colorful displays on the open squares. Perhaps she will find just the flowers she wants at the nearest street corner. It is a common practice in Sweden to bring a bouquet when calling on friends, as mentioned in another connection, and it is considered quite proper to come with a very small tribute of flowers, three roses, for instance, or carnations. A first visit calls for a more elaborate bouquet, however. Most Swedish homes have potted plants in the windows, often geraniums, and outside the buildings there are flower boxes lending color to the façade. Public places are made attractive with luxurious foliage plants. Even railroad stations are decked with bright flowers planted in suspended baskets. Parks as well as private gardens abound with flower beds showing floral designs in contrasting colors.

The third of the fundamental characteristics of a Swede is, according to the professor, *"ganska hyggliga."* According to the dictionary it means to be "well-behaved, respectable, kind, good, decent, agreeable, nice, reasonable, moderate." Are we of Swedish descent all that? Suppose we take the professor's word for it while we try to live up to each of the qualifications.

How about traits of the opposite kind? However much we would like to think of ourselves as *ganska hyggliga,* there still must be qualities of less merit. Gustav Sundbärg (1857-1914), a renowned statistician, points them out in *Det svenska folklynnet* (The Swedish Temperament), an analysis of the cause of the Swedish emigration to America, published at the beginning of this century. He claims that the Swede lacks psychological insight which prevents him from learning to know himself and others. Even writers lack knowledge of human nature, he says. "Selma Lagerlöf has given us Sweden's nature and Sweden's animal kingdom, but where are Sweden's people?" Gustav Sundbärg in his book claims further that only duty towards king and country lie at the base of his feelings for his native land, not patriotism; also that he, while working hard and painstakingly, is ignorant of gainful economic calculations and that he has a weakness for anything of a foreign nature. He also speaks of *den kungliga svenska avundsjukan* (the royal Swedish envy). Does all this seem unreasonable, or is there a grain of truth in the claims?

Looking at the Swedes objectively, a foreign visitor in Sweden often writes home of his observations, and it is to be assumed that they reflect his true feelings. A French woman stated recently that in Sweden THINGS had reached perfection, but how about the Swedes themselves, she wonders. The social problems are solved, she continues, but the individual seems unhappy, dissatisfied. The Swedes' concern about justice and equality in civil service jobs, in manufacturing plants, in the school system, seems to fill the working time with worry and tension and jeopardizes personal happiness.

A Frenchman who has taught French in Sweden for a number of years says that the Swede is reserved (we have heard that before!), not socially proud, and sincere. Side by side in his classes sit a bus driver, a countess, a postal clerk, an ambassador's daughter, a college principal, and others, all taking a lively part in discussions. They never hesitate to criticize others' political views, says the Frenchman. But ask him or her to express something in French and they are silent. Being a perfectionist, a Swede does not want to take a chance, unless he is sure of the answer. One of the male students had been particularly reticent in trying out French phrases. One evening when the French instructor became ill a doctor was called, and who should step into the room but the shy student from the class. He is one of Sweden's top physicians, well-known to a great many—except to the Frenchman who taught him French.

A British diplomat who has lived in Sweden for three years was interviewed before his departure for another post. What were his likes and dislikes? "We like Swedish food," he said, "and as you can see here in our home we like Swedish textiles. If I must be mean I could say that you are perfectionists and protocol-minded—and too modest. We have marvelled at the glowing health of your political personages who can sit through a night of discussion and come forth in the morning with a sane, well-balanced statement of their findings."

A common complaint about the Swede is that he

seldom answers letters. Many a foreign business man who repeatedly has requested information by mail finds it more expedient to make a trip to Sweden and find out for himself what he wants to know. Personal correspondence is something else, but it, too, is often neglected. It is suggested that the main reason why Swedes are slow in writing letters is the lack of a standard form or pattern to go by. English-speaking people who can begin any letter to any one with "Dear Sir" or "Dear Mr. Jones" have no appreciation of the dilemma facing a Swede when he is to compose a letter. Shall he write *Bästa, Kära,* or *Ärade?* Undecided, he postpones the ordeal until it seems embarrassing to write at all, and the letter remains unanswered. In personal correspondence form and style are usually not the delaying reason. One often hears: "I have nothing to write about." Children away from home have perhaps not succeeded as well as anticipated and the letter home is difficult to write. And parents look in vain. . . . Silently they waited in generations past for that letter from America which never came.

# THERE IS A MUSICAL STRAIN . . .

# THERE IS A MUSICAL STRAIN . . .

When attempting to bring into the limelight some of the characteristics of a Swede, one realizes that it is only possible to catch a glimpse of his true nature. This is indeed the case when an attempt is made to talk of his love of music, which here must be limited to his love of song and melody. The musical tradition of Sweden is rich in *visor* or songs of a light timbre and the enjoyment of singing them is a national pastime. University male choruses have for generations contributed in great measure to Swedish song, and presented it at a high level of performance. Singing societies have greeted spring in open-air concerts year after year and continue to salute king and citizenry on a number of special occasions.

Music has always played a great role in the life of the Swedish people. The older generation responded warmly to the magnificent voices of Jenny Lind (1820-1887) and Christina Nilsson (1843-1921), while their descendants have enjoyed hearing the silver voice of Jussi Björling, born in 1911, who for a number of years gladdened the world with his song until his career was cut short in 1960. Birgit Nilsson (1918-    ), Sweden's contemporary soprano, is acclaimed and applauded in America as well as in her own country and in Europe for her operatic roles.

"Do you like music?" Sometimes we cannot say because there is such a variety of it. Sometimes the musical

strain lies dormant until one day a tune will strike a
corresponding chord and begin to stir the senses. All at
once one feels alive with the enjoyment of it and something
worthwhile has been added to one's experience of music.
"Yes, I do love a singing melody," is often the answer to the
question.

Going back in time to more primitive living, a tune
could be of practical import, and is to this day, for instance
in Dalarna and regions farther north, where it is the practice each spring to bring the cattle from the farm up to the
mountains above. The young woman who is tending the
cattle for the summer lives in a cottage called *fäbod*. By
blowing a tune in a cowherd's horn or *lur,* a kind of
trumpet often made of birch bark, she can summon the
cows. They are accustomed to respond to the mournful
sound. Such tunes are called *vallåtar*. The mountain slope,
where the grass is usually greener and more lush than at
any other place on the farm, is a favorite spot for the
animals who reciprocate by giving more and richer milk,
which in turn produces butter and cheese under the busy
fingers of the milkmaid. Often in the evenings she com-
municates with her neighbor over on another mountain
slope by calling a tune on the trumpet. The melody echoes
across the bluff. She listens. Soon there is a tune in response. Such an exchange of greetings helps to dispel the
sense of loneliness. Nowadays, there is often more than
one woman living at the cottage. A warning signal from
the trumpet will also notify the home folks in the valley
of an emergency.

These primitive airs have been used as themes for processional bridal music, drinking songs, and other incidental
music, and have in many instances served as motifs for
modern classical and popular compositions.

As mentioned before, the Swedes love to sing and many

are the occasions when they lift their voices in vigorous outpouring. The fullbodied participation in the singing at a church service, for instance, demonstrates this inclination. Incidentally, some Swedish congregations develop their own style of singing and a zealous organist, bent on following his notes, may have difficulty in bringing voices and music together. It is reported that in Mora church in Dalarna the people sing after their own fashion, especially hymn number 424 in the State Church hymnal—*"Den signade dag"* (The Blessed Day)—which is considered their very own. They sing all nine stanzas and with accelerated fervor. It has been called a *koral i sockendräkt* (a hymn in parish dress) and the melody with which it is sung is strictly that of the Mora people. Those who remember Finn-Karin, who died in 1912, say that her clear, strong voice carried the melody above all others and that the congregation followed her devotedly in all her fanciful digressions. Efforts have been made to eradicate the tuneful pirouettes and frills and make the melody "straight", but they have failed. The Mora people still sing the hymn in their own way.

Instrumental folk music that previously lived in the memory from generation to generation was never recorded. In Sweden today there is great concern for the preservation of the old tunes and several folk music historians are occupied with the task. A substantial collection of these tunes has now been compiled. Through contests and organizations of folk music societies, a lively interest in this living musical culture has been aroused.

It is a great event in Sweden when a team of fiddlers and accordion players gather for a contest and play their favorite music. The tapping of toes indicates the listeners' animated participation. Such music is equally relished when performed by only one or two players at a Saturday night dance in an open dance pavilion, or on a sturdy dock by the seashore. In times past every parish, at least in Dalarna and Värmland, had its self-taught *spelman,* it seems, who could be called on to play at weddings and funerals, as well as at a dance. He was often a moody, sensitive fellow who would rather sit under the flowering lilac bush in the spring playing his instrument than to participate in the common farm chores. His music was often sad, his tunes reflecting something of his own dissatisfaction with life and his yearning for self-expression. He played from within the deep wells of his soul, sometimes improvising, at other times following the well-known melody of an old folk song. On festive occasions he would close his own treasure chest of tunes and comply with the general request for lilting dance melodies. He knew how to play these, too. He knew what was suitable at a wedding, and he knew what was fitting to play at a funeral. Naturally, he was considered odd, not wanting to till the soil, not wanting to be part of the tasks performed around him.

The highly gifted woodsman and poet Dan Andersson (1888-1920), who wrote many of his hauntingly beautiful lyrics while tending a charcoal kiln in southern Dalarna, has in his poem *"Spelmannen"* portrayed such a fiddler, and in another poem called *"En spelmans jordafärd"* (A Fiddler's Last Journey), he describes how the four mourners on their way to the grave carry the black coffin across the hillside scattered with wild roses, while they quietly comment on the loneliness and misery that their departed friend had endured. Their heavy boots tread on and crush the delicate rose petals until they bleed. "Ah, a king," the roses murmur and are tramped upon again, "a king— and a dreamer too, is dead." This quotation is taken from Caroline Schleef's translation of the poem included in her publication *Charcoal-Burner's Ballad and Other Poems.*

In Sweden's cultural tradition there may be traced in many a lighthearted creation a tender, bittersweet sadness, expressed in poetry as well as in music. Even Carl Michael Bellman (1740-1795), the seemingly carefree, high-spirited, convivial troubadour of his time, had a marked strain of melancholy in his nature. With his brilliant gift for words and music he made others laugh while he himself often harbored sadness in his soul.

Esaias Tegnér (1782-1846), one of Sweden's romantic poets, caught this trend in Bellman's temperament with the classic lines:

*Märk det vemodsdraget över pannan,*
*ett nordiskt sångardrag, en sorg i rosenrött.*

(Note the tinge of sadness over his forehead,
a Nordic keynote of song, a rose-hued sorrow).

Most Bellman songs, however, are a happy blend of lyrics and melody, forming a unique entity which makes them delightful to sing. There are few Swedes who do not know several of the Bellman melodies, and everybody knows:

*Gubben Noak, gubben Noak,*
*var en hedersman.*
*När han gick ur arken*
*plantera' han på marken*
*mycket vin, ja, mycket vin, ja,*
*detta gjorde han.*

There are eight stanzas to this song, but it is only the first one that seems to be imprinted on the Swedish mind. Bellman's skillful play on words makes is difficult to translate accurately. The pun on *vin,* meaning wine, must here be rendered with the word vine, which bears the grape that produces the wine!

Therefore, the complete translation would be:

Old man Noah, old man Noah
was an honorable man.
When he left the ark
he planted in the ground
many vines, yes, many vines, yes,
this indeed he did.

Due to the difficulty of catching the true meaning of
the words of Bellman, this beloved Swedish poet has not
been made known in America, at least not to any great
extent. On his visits to Sweden the late American historian
Hendrik van Loon (1882-1944) became so fascinated
with the lyrics and music of Bellman that he decided to
attempt an interpretation of some of his songs. The
result was the entertainingly rendered *The Last of the
Troubadours,* imaginatively illustrated by the author. The
musical arrangements of the twenty songs are done by
Grace Castagnetta.

A strong advocate of Bellman lore in America today
is the acclaimed Danish lieder singer, Aksel Schiötz, whose
contributions to a better knowledge of this great poet and
composer are considerable. And a young American-born
ballad singer, William Clauson, who came to Sweden at
the age of two, has during his voice studies there, as
well as in this country, developed a rare ability for
interpreting Bellman.

Is it true that at the bottom of the Swedish folk
temperament there is a recess of melancholy? At least,
that seems to be the opinion of the judges giving their final
verdict in a contest held in Sweden recently. Radio listeners
had voted on ten of the most popular melodies from the
international world of song, giving *"När ljusen tändas
därhemma"* (When It Is Lamplighting Time in the Valley)
the highest number of votes. The next one in popularity

was *"Barndomshemmet"* (Childhood Home) and the third *"O, solo mio,"* the well-known Neapolitan song. Other popular tunes were "Ramona," "In My Sweet Little Alice Blue Gown," in Swedish called *"I min blommiga blå krinolin,"* and "Lili Marlene." It was established by the judges that the most popular tunes were those that sobbed and sighed and whose text dealt with red lakeside cottages, birch groves, wheat fields glistening in the sunset, memories of mother, or a tearful tale of lost love. Many of the songs chosen have originated in America, later to become popular in Sweden through a cleverly worded translation that blends well with the melody.

Had the contest dealt with purely Swedish melodies, the old folk songs surely would have had a place among the top numbers. They never cease to capture the imagination of singing societies and individual singers alike and are often favorite numbers on concert programs when Swedish performances are given abroad. It is true that many of these folk songs are in the minor key, such as *"Vårvindar friska"* (Fresh Spring Breezes), *"Ack, Värmeland, du sköna"* (O, Värmeland, Thou Beautiful), *"Kristallen den fina"* (Crystal Fine), and others. Folk songs of this caliber are in a category of their own, having become a part of the musical tradition of Sweden. They stand the test of time.

In spite of the great popularity in Sweden today of the recordings of American "top tunes," especially among the younger generation, folk songs and *visor* continue to capture and hold the interest of genuine music lovers throughout the land. *Visor* is a category of Swedish songs that perhaps could be called ballads in miniature, set to simple, uncomplicated but engaging melodies. The word *visa,* which is the singular form, can also be compared with an Old English "air". What especially distinguishes *visor* from other types of song are the lyrics. The words, which usually present pictures of idyllic settings in which the personages appear, often reveal poetry of quality and they enhance and "carry" the melody.

In Sweden today there is a distinguished association called *Visans Vänner* (Friends of *Visan*) whose members get together for the sheer fun of singing and rediscovering and composing *visor*. These music lovers do not only sing with love in their hearts but aim at interpreting the words, to dramatize the story of the songs they sing. Bellman's songs are favorites, naturally, but also those of today such as are written and composed by the popular contemporary poet Evert Taube (pronounced Tohb), in Sweden sometimes called "the troubadour of our time." His delightful *"Calle Schevens vals"* which has all the earmarks of a *visa,* has become so popular that it can be characterized as folk music. The son, Sven-Bertil Taube, noted recording artist and actor, has also become popular as a singer of *visor.* It is customary to accompany these songs on a guitar or a lute.

A traditional little tune for singing at a birthday celebration or at any other occasion when someone is to be honored is this familiar song:

Ja, må han (hon) leva, ja, må han leva,
Ja, må han leva uti hundrade år!
Ja, visst ska han leva, ja, visst ska han leva,
Ja, visst ska han leva, uti hundrade år!


Och när han har levat, och när han har levat,
Och när han har levat uti hundrade år,
Ja, då ska han leva, ja, då ska han leva,
Ja, då ska han leva uti hundrade år!

This is a repeated wish that the celebrant may live
to be a hundred, and when he has reached that ripe old
age, well, then he shall live—to be a hundred! Fancy that!

The lyric strain in the make-up of a Swede, be it in
poetry or melody, comes to light wherever he lives, and
those who emigrated and settled in America found expression for their joy or disappointment in the immigrant
ballads. Some of these ballads reflect a sentimental, plain-
tive mood giving air to nostalgia and loneliness, whereas
others express a robust, frivolous humor. Often they paint
a picture of America as the land flowing with milk and
honey, the land where gold could be carved out with jack-
knives. That there was another side to the picture—discovered once the settlers came to live in this new country
—is also depicted. Although pride kept the majority of
immigrants from leaving the life they had chosen, there
was an occasional return to the old country, as recorded
in one of the most popular ballads of the time, namely
*"Petter Jönssons Amerika-resa."* It tells of Petter's disgust
with the order of things in Sweden, with the deceit and
fraud of the officials as revealed in *Fäderneslandet,* a semi-
weekly newspaper that attacked aristocracy and capitalism,
advocated drastic social reforms, and finally degen-
erated into a foul scandal sheet. He left his small hometown,
Trosa, popularly referred to as the end of the world, and
set out on his trip to America.

The ballad which describes Petter's adventures over
the Atlantic and his immediate return in Trosa, was
written in 1872 by Magnus Henrik Elmblad (1848-1888),
a Swedish journalist, who after a few years of study at
Uppsala University came to Chicago, where he found em-
ployment with Swedish language newspapers. While regarded in the United States as the foremost poet among
the Swedish-Americans, his literary production is now quite

forgotten, with the exception of this ballad. It has appeared in collections of folk songs both in this country and in Sweden and was sung to an old popular melody, which during the years has been used for a number of other songs. Petter Jönsson, who in America became Peter Johnson, has been the source of amusement among Swedish-speaking people in this country for almost a century and it has been sung to the accompaniment of an accordion, a mouth organ, or a fiddle wherever Swedes gathered.

The following presentation of the ballad, in its entirety, appears in modern spelling.

PETTER JÖNSSONS AMERIKA-RESA
Och Petter Jönsson han såg i Fäderneslandet,
Att ämbetsmännen förstört det nordiska landet,
Då blev han ledsen och tänkte: "Jäkeln anamma:
Jag tror jag kilar min väg med detsamma."

Han tog sin plunta och stoppa' matsäck i kistan,
Och av polisen hans namn blev uppsatt på listan,
Ur vänstra ögat han strök bort tåren med vanten,
Tog Gud i hågen och gav sig ut på Atlanten.

Han ville bort till det stora landet i väster,
Där ingen kung finns och inga kitsliga präster,
Där får man sova och äta fläsk och potatis,
Och se'n med flottet kan smörja stövlarna gratis.

Där ingen länsman törs stöta bonden för pannan,
Och renat brännvin kan fås för sex styver kannan,
Där mera pengar det finns än loppor i Trosa—
Dit ville Petter och dit han styrde sin kosa.

På skeppet stod han och liksom höll sig för magen
Förty hans själ var av mycken ångest betagen.
Det stod ej till att gå ned och lägga sig heller;
Ty stormen blåser som bara hin när det gäller.

Ett gudslån (om man ej räknar oxstek och limpa)
Han ej fått i sig och våt han var som en simpa,
Uti sitt förskinn han utgöt hela sin suckan
Och snyfta' bittert: "Ack, den som vore vid luckan!"

I våta byxor han stod vid masten och lipa'!
Det var så kallt så att magen började knipa!
Då kom en båtsman tog Petter Jönsson i nacken,
Liksom en hundvalp och slängde ner'en på "backen".

Där låg nu Petter, och vattnet skvalade om'en.
Och själv han trodde hans sista timme var kommen.
Men båtsman skratta' och ropade i hans öra:
"Vad tusan skulle du på galejan att göra?"

Men stormen tystna' och solen sken över skutan,
Då vakna' Petter och trilla' ner i kajutan.
Han tog en långsup, tog två, kröp ned under täcket
Och på tre veckor han se'n ej syntes på däcket.

Först när i New York på redden skutan låg inne,
Kröp Petter fram, ack—men magerlagd som en pinne.
Med sorgsna blickar han mätte förskinnets stroppar
Och bad för Guds skull om några koleradroppar.

I Castle-garden han slog sig ner vid sin kista,
Och åt och drack så han kunde andan sin mista.
Så bar han kista och alltihop till en jude
Som sa': "Mein herr, firti Thaler kan jak wohl bjude."

Men Petter Jönsson till hamnen styrde sin kosa,
Och da'n därpå reste han tillbaka till Trosa.
Och förr skall solen väl spricka sönder i kanten
Än Petter Jönsson far ut igen på Atlanten!

The following translation is by E. Gustav Johnson,
professor emeritus, North Park College, the official archi-
vist of the Evangelical Covenant Church of America,
curator of the archives at North Park, and secretary
and editor of *The Swedish Pioneer Historical Quarterly.*
Both the Swedish and the English texts are taken from the
November 1948 issue of the *Scandinavian Studies.*

### PETER JOHNSON'S TRIP TO AMERICA
And Peter Johnson he read in "The Fatherland"
That bureaucrats had ruined the northern land.
He got disgusted and thought: "The devil take it!
I guess I'll hurry away and that immediately."

He took his hip flask and stowed some lunch in a chest
And by the police his name was enrolled on the list.
From the left eye he wiped a tear with his mitten,
With God in mind he set forth upon the Atlantic.

He would away to the great land in the west,
Where there is no king and no squeamish priests:
Where one may sleep and eat pork and potatoes,
And then with the grease smear one's boots gratis.

Where no sheriff dares knock a farmhand on the head,
And distilled whiskey may be had for six pence a quart.
Where more money is found than fleas in Trosa—
Thither would Peter go, and thither he steered his course.

On the ship he stood and kind of held on to his belly,
Because his soul was with great anguish beset.
There was no use to go below and lie down either,
For the storm blew like the very devil, for that matter.

Not the least bit (if you don't count beefsteak and pumper-
      nickel)
Had he eaten, and wet he was as a sponge.
In his wrapper he muffled all of his sighing
And sobbed bitterly: "Oh, if one were only at the trap
      door!"

In wet breeches he stood by the mast whimpering;
It was terribly cold, and his stomach began to pinch!
Then came a sailor and took Peter Johnson by the neck
Just like a cur and flung him down on the deck.

There now lay Peter and the water swished about him,
He thought himself that his last hour had come.
But the sailor laughed and shouted in his ear:
"What the hell did you board this galley for?"

The storm it calmed and the sun it shone o'er the schooner,
Then Peter wakened and rolled down into the cabin.
He took a long drink—took two—crept under the blanket,
And for three weeks he was no more seen on deck.

Not till the schooner, in New York, lay at the pier
Did Peter crawl out, but oh, as skinny as a rail!
With doleful eyes he measured the belt of his breeches,
And asked, for God's sake, for some cholera drops.

In Castle Garden he dropped down alongside his chest
And ate and drank so that he nearly lost his breath.
Then he toted his chest and everything to a Jew
Who said: "Mein Herr! Forty dollars I can offer you."

Then Peter Johnson down to the port steered his course,
And the next day he journeyed back to Trosa.
And rather likely the sun will split at the edges,
Ere Peter Johnson again ventures out on the Atlantic.

**A TITLE IS VITAL**

# A TITLE IS VITAL

The Swedes themselves admit that they suffer from *titelsjuka,* by which they mean an unwholesome predilection for titles. In spite of sincere efforts by level-headed individuals to lift the bond of formality in this peculiar situation, the custom persists. *Herr* is used in addressing a gentleman when no other title can be conjured forth, but it has an aura of inadequacy. In all fairness, titles do aid in identification. As included with the names in telephone directories they facilitate the search for a number, especially when the name is a common one. But one must know by which title the person is listed. In a long line of Anderssons, for instance, it helps if you know that the person in question is a lawyer, in Swedish *advokat,* the titles being listed alphabetically. Going down the listings of Anderssons with titles from a to ö (ö being the last letter of the Swedish alphabet), one finally comes to occupations like *överste*—colonel—or perhaps *ölutkörare*, meaning a beer truck driver. After all the ö-jobs are exhausted, there follows a listing of Anderssons with street addresses only. It is hard to say whether these persons have failed to acquire a trade or professional title, or simply prefer to have only names and addresses listed.

Also, in social life a title has an identifying purpose. It establishes class and rank, line of work, and level of education. In an introduction *Herr* Holm fails to carry the weight as does *direktör* Holm. The title *direktör* has a high-sounding ring, establishing a facade of respectability and social worth. A Swede would immediately fit him into his niche as a manufacturer, a business executive, or a store owner of some consequence. The title has many handles. Another influential title is *disponent,* ordinarily given to a manager of an industry, or enterprise of note. Other titles identfy a *rektor* as a president of a college, an *ingeniör* in the field of engineering, a *författare* as an author, and so forth.

To be caught in the tangle of long titles can be quite embarrassing, as is told by a Swedish journalist who was sent to interview *ecklesiastikministern*—the minister of education. The long word simply stuck in his throat. After numerous attempts, he abbreviated it to *ministern.* Suddenly it struck him that he could use the far simpler title *stadsråd* —cabinet minister—but made the fatal mistake of calling the distinguished gentleman *stadsbudet*—meaning porter! Such an incident can happen only in a country where the language lacks an expedient word for *you.*

The Swedes have tried to establish a word of address that would be equally suitable, but to no avail. *Ni* has proved an unbecoming word and is ordinarily used only when speaking to a person whose name and title is not known. In speaking to two or more people it is acceptable to say *ni,* however, if one does not want to use the formal word *herrskapet.* Those who defy custom and good taste and use *ni* when addressing a person whose name and title they know, often find themselves in an isolated situation with few persons to say it to. Writers write about the so called *"ni-frågan,"* linguists come up with suggestions in attempts to establish a word acceptable to all concerned, and the common man shrugs his shoulders and continues to struggle with titles. But usually he avoids a personal approach and speaks in a circumscribed way.

There is a deep-rooted reason why the word *ni,* addressed to one person, is shunned among Swedes of fastidious language habits. There is an aura of condescension about it, whether the person using it intends it or not. Even uttered in a guileless manner it can cause irritation, as in the incident of a Swedish woman who, picking up a scarf from the street, turned to a man standing by and said: *"Har ni tappat den här?"* (Have you dropped this?) The man tossed his head and snapped: *"Jag är inte ni för er!"* The gist of his outburst was: "I won't stand for your calling me '*ni*'!" Had the woman used a more careful wording: *"Har min herre tappat den här?"* she would have escaped the biting response.

This is only one case, however. No doubt other individuals would have responded with less ire, dismissing the matter with a shrug. The sting would be felt, nevertheless. To an older, sensitive Swede the word still jars. The only group that uses *ni* without hesitation, it seems, is the Swedish youth. And if young people upon meeting begin calling each other *ni,* they soon will replace it with the more familiar *du.* In most instances they say *du* from the start.

In an article on the subject, the noted professor Herbert Tingsten (1896-     ), formerly editor-in-chief of *Dagens Nyheter,* Sweden's largest liberal newspaper, gives his opinion thus: "I think it sounds far more friendly to address a student (university) *kandidaten* (the candidate) than to say *ni* to him." Needless to say, the students addressed Mr. Tingsten *professorn.*

In earlier times it was often customary that persons of higher rank used *han* and *hon*—he and she—in speaking to those of lesser eminence. The story is told of King Oscar

II (1829-1907), who at one time visited the anatomical institution in Uppsala and how he during his round encountered a medical student occupied in dissecting a corpse. Addressing the student, the king asked: *"Tycker han inte att det är ganska obehagligt?"* (Does he not think it is quite unpleasant?) The answer came quickly: "No, Your Majesty. He is dead!"

Is there a way out? Many are the suggestions and many are the efforts made to find a solution—as mentioned before. One is the magic little word *du*. This is the personal pronoun used among relatives and friends. With relatives it is more or less automatic. With others it must be achieved. Before arriving at the *du* stage, there are conditions to be met. Before the older person, or higher ranked, suggests the shedding of titles and henceforth the use of first names, he will calculate and weigh the matter, because once the step is taken there is no return. In Sweden one may have many acquaintances—friends are chosen. And the gulf between is considerable.

The moment two Swedes arrive at the speaking term of *du* they shake hands. They have now literally—and socially—stepped closer to one another. The incident often comes about at a gathering when a few drinks have relaxed tension and the atmosphere is geared to friendly relations. In earlier times drinking *duskål* was quite a ceremony. Arms were linked and in that awkward position the drink was emptied. For an added climax the glasses were often thrown into the fireplace, the grand gesture followed by joyous shouts and loud cheers. Nowadays the ceremony is simplified. Facing each other with lifted glasses, the two participants gaze into each others eyes. They drink. A short bow follows and they are *du*.

In some instances a third person, called *fadder* or sponsor, assumes the role of go-between for the purpose

of getting the two people together, who for some reason
have failed to arrive at the concluding *du* stage. Between
men of the same profession and social status the *du* is
in most cases established upon meeting, making them
"brothers" at once. In letters they will salute each other
*Bäste Bror,* sometimes abbreviated to "B. B." In groups
of students and athletes, workers in the same industry,
members of the military forces and of the same political
party, and similar associations it is customary to slip into
the *du* status at first contact. And it is becoming more and
more common even in other social groups.

Women seem to be more discriminating in their choice
of *du* mates. They may work in an office for a long time
before letting down the bar. A nurse has the professional
title *syster* (sister). Say that her name is Karin Berg, for
instance, she will be called *syster Karin.* A story is told
about a young nurse being on duty at a hospital where the
noted caricaturist and professor of art Albert Engström
(1869-1940) was a patient. It was her first day and
stepping into his room, she curtsied and introduced herself
as *syster Karin.* The ailing professor raised himself up in
bed, made an attempt at bowing, and smiled. *Bror Albert*
(brother Albert), he said with a glint in his eye.

An elementary public school teacher in Sweden is
a *folkskollärarinna* (the masculine title is *folkskollärare*),
but her pupils call her *fröken* (miss). By marriage a
woman will acquire the feminine form of her husband's
title. A doctor's wife becomes *doktorinnan,* a professor's
wife *professorskan.* Married to a man of nobility—*friherre*
(baron) or *greve* (count)—she will be addressed *friher-
rinnan* or *grevinnan,* respectively. However, the most common title for a married woman is *fru* (Mrs.). Unmarried
women are called *fröken.* Social form demands that the
title is followed by the name. In times past, when some

Swedish households had domestic help the lady of the house was addressed *frun*. The master of the house was called *herrn*.

Younger people usually address their mother's women friends *tant* (aunt) followed by the first name, and their father's friends *farbror* (uncle), that is, if they have not been invited to say "*du*." Sons and daughters-in-law often use these designations to their respective parents-in-law, although many say *mor* and *far* (mother and father). The old forms *svärmor* (mother-in-law) and *svärfar* (father-in-law) are disappearing.

When one is in doubt what to call an elderly country woman, one often resorts to *mor* or *moster* (the latter actually meaning aunt on your mother's side but used formerly as *tant* is used today). It is far more friendly to say *mor Anna* or *moster Stava* than to say *ni* or *hon*. But with modern trends the use of *fru* will no doubt be extended to embrace every married woman regardless of status. At least, the leveling process is going on.

Swedish children say *mamma* and *pappa* or *mor* and *far* to their parents, but just as often they say *du*. This was unheard of a few generations ago. Far back in time children were obliged to say *I* to their elders. And from such verb-forms as *hafven I* (have you) or *kunnen I* (can you) a solecism was developed, namely the berated word *ni*, which since has been treated as a stepchild. Perhaps in time it will be fully accepted and bring fluency to the spoken word.

The inhabitants of Dalarna have maintained the use of the original *du* throughout times. They have said *du* to rich and poor, young and old, even to the king himself. There were no frills but direct speech when the dala-men responded to King Gustaf Vasa's proposals and decrees, and through the succeeding generations this independent spirit has lived on, although today tempered by new blood and new images.

How does an instructor of Swedish succeed in teaching the *du* and *ni* forms to American students? She doesn't! What remains is to impress upon them the importance of not saying *du* to strangers and mere acquaintances when visiting in Sweden—and then let the *ni*'s fall where ever they may!

## A SIP OR TWO

# A SIP OR TWO

Coffee is essential to the majority of Swedes, whether it comes in the forenoon or in the afternoon or after dinner. Swedish people do not drink coffee with their dinner—it comes after the meal and is served in another room, often before an open fire or with candles lighted. *Kaffe på maten* denotes relaxation—a moment of the day dedicated to pleasant talk and friendly chats.

There was a time in Sweden, however, when coffee was a rare drink indeed. In 1657, when an ambassador to king Karl X Gustaf returned from Turkey, where he had been sent on some political mission, he reported having been compelled to drink a bitter concoction offered to him. He had looked at the black drink with apprehension, he said, but learned to drink it "without burning myself."

When the first bag of coffee beans came to Göteborg in 1685, there were few buyers. No one seemed to know how to use the product, and for some time it was considered a corrective, a remedy. It is told how Carl von Linné (1707-1778), the world-renowned botanist and zoologist, also professor of medicine, one morning after his round of calls at a hospital ship became nauseated from the bad odor of the patients, and how he ordered strong coffee, drank three cups of it, and "recovered at once."

Coffee was first served in coffee houses, and it has been estimated that in 1728 there were fifteen such places

in Stockholm. They were at first the favorite haunts of
sailors, traveling merchants, and soldiers of fortune but
were later frequented by poets and troubadours as well.
Slowly the coffee-drinking habit penetrated into the
Swedish homes. Anna Maria Lenngren (1754-1817)
relates in her poem *"Den glada festen"* (The happy celebration) that already in the morning *prostfar* (clergyman)
had been treated to coffee that was *"utvalt gott"* (exceptionally good).

The enjoyment of coffee caused a Mauritz Cramaer
(1818-1846) to expound its excellence in verse and this
"ode" to coffee became very popular through the years.
Snatches of it were often repeated, and many a Swedish-
American has heard a grandmother or aunt recite the
words over a cup of coffee. Numerous times I have been
asked for a copy of these lyrics, and a few years ago an
executive of an instant coffee firm in New York wrote
to the Department of Scandinavian at the University of
Minnesota requesting it. As a young boy in Minnesota
he had heard his mother sing "a rollicking Swedish song
about coffee," he wrote. Could we possibly send him the
words? As far as he could remember, he concluded, the
translation would run something like this:

"A cup of coffee is the best drink in the whole world,
It braces the body and strengthens the soul,
And thrills one's whole being from the head
All the way down to one's toes."

By that time I had succeeded in obtaining from Sweden
a copy of the complete text and was delighted that I could
supply it. Some time later I was pleasantly surprised to
receive from the executive in New York a recording of
the music to the lyrics, and a letter telling that a "kind

Swedish vice consul" in the East had written out the melody
lines from memory and that an organist had arranged the
tune and recorded the music. The writer expressed amazement that the melody was in a minor mode, because he
had recalled it was a jolly tune. In this case it was just
too bad, as it would bar it from any commercial use in
jingles!

Here follows the complete text to the acclaimed *visa*.
In the first version that I obtained the refrain was *"hå, hå,
ja, ja,"* but in checking the original edition of *Femhundra
Riksdaler Banco* at the city library in Stockholm I found
that the refrain was *Halleluja*.

### HYLLNINGSDIKT TILL KAFFET

Av allt det goda som man förtär
Bland alla jordiska drycker
Ju kaffetåren den bästa är.
Den skingrar människans nycker,
Den styrker kroppen och livar själen,
Den känns från hjässan, ja, ned i hälen.

                                        Halleluja.

När hösten kommer med blåst och snö,
När våren börjar sin väta,
Då blir till lynnet man kärv och slö,
Man blott vill sova och träta.
Ja, man blir ruskig i hela kroppen,
Men . . . då finns hälsan i kaffekoppen!

                                        Halleluja.

När frun sin älskade man har mist
Och sitter ensam med gälden,
Hon bittert sörjer sin dubbla brist,
Men sätter pannan på elden:
Och när den klarnat hon lämnar båren
Och hämtar styrka i kaffetåren.

                                        Halleluja.

När färska nyheter månde tas
Från stadens hundrade kanter,
Man på ett litet honett kalas
Ser sina vänner och tanter . . .
Vid kaffebordet man gör sitt bästa
Med fantiserande om sin nästa.

Halleluja.

Den ena dricker sin tår på bit,
En annan älskar att doppa,
Parlerar därvid med sådan flit
Att man bör öronen proppa.
Som trumman mullrar vid krigsreveljen
Så bullrar tungorna i konseljen.

Halleluja.

Förutan kaffe—o, gudadryck,
Vad vore mänskliga livet!
Allt nytt som ännu ej finns i tryck
I pannans botten står skrivet:
Ty sen man druckit ur sista slumpen,
Stå livets gåtor i kaffesumpen!

Halleluja.

The translation that follows is simply a line by line
interpretation.

Of all the good things that one consumes,
among all the worldly drinks,
the coffee sip is the very best.
It disperses the whims of men,
it fortifies the body and quickens the mind.
One feels it from the head down to the heel.

Halleluja.

When fall comes with wind and snow,
when spring begins its rains,
then one becomes bleak and dull.
All one wants to do is to sleep and quibble.
Yes, one's whole body is out of sorts,
but then . . . there is health in the coffee cup!

> Halleluja.

When the wife has lost her beloved husband
and sits alone with the debts,
she bitterly mourns her twofold plight
but puts the coffee pot on the fire.
And when the coffee is clear she leaves the bier
and gets strength in a sip of coffee.

> Halleluja.

When the latest news be gathered in
from the city's hundred sources,
at a small nice party
one would see one's friends and intimates.
At the coffee table one does the very best
gossiping about the neighbors.

> Halleluja.

One would suck her lump of sugar with the coffee,
another would love to dip the bread,
meanwhile talking with such force
that the ears ought to be plugged.
Just as the drums roar at an army camp
the tongues clamor at the conference.

> Halleluja.

Without coffee—oh, heavenly drink,
what would human life be!
All the news not yet in print
stands written in the bottom of the pot:
Because after the last drop is gone
life's riddles are "solved" in the coffee grounds!

> Halleluja.

As it says in the fifth stanza, coffee drinking habits of old included *"dricka på bit,"* which meant sipping coffee while a lump of sugar slowly melted on the tongue. Pouring the coffee on the saucer, blowing on it, and lapping it up from the rim was another custom indulged in by a majority of people, although frowned upon in some circles, naturally. Capriciously depicted in cartoons, such scenes have become a relished part of folk humor, and the name that comes to mind particularly is Albert Engström, the late caricaturist, who with a few bold lines could portray a situation that struck to the core. He was the popular illustrator in *Strix,* a humor magazine of consequence (no longer published).

Coffee parties, called *kafferep* or *kaffekalas,* embrace a custom that has long traditions and continue to play an important role in Swedish social life. For every birthday and name day of family and friends, guests gather around the coffee table for a celebration. It is important to a housewife's good name that she upholds the tradition and serves the customary seven kinds of cookies, in addition to the substantial coffee bread, which is served first and humorously called *grovdoppa.* Each guest must partake of every kind of *småbröd* (cookies). Lastly, the pièce de résistance is brought in—the birthday cake or name day cake. It is often ordered from a confectionary shop and is beautifully decorated with glazed fruit and marzipan, filled with either a creamy custard, jam, or whip cream.

At one time in my lettuce days, I was invited to a coffee party in a wealthy farm home in Småland. The table was decked out with such an abundance of cookies and small cakes that it was beyond human capacity to eat more than a part of them. Nevertheless, we were coaxed to fill the plates with a sample of each kind. In amused disbelief we held up the heaped up cookies before the smiling hostess. She pointed to a small table where stacks of paper bags were piled up. "Eat what you can and take the rest with you home," she said. So we did and walked home with a goodly assortment of cookies, which later was distributed among the youngsters at home. Such overabundance is not practiced in Sweden today, I am sure.

But still persistent is the custom of standing on ceremony when it comes to approaching the coffee table. An awareness of rank is in evidence because no one precedes the first lady of the parish, which in the country would be the clergyman's wife, or any lady of social prominence. It is proper to be modest and stand back awaiting one's turn, according to prestige and rank, and in spite of the hostess' solicitous coaxing and tugging, there is often delayed action—while the coffee cools in the coffee cups. This is called *att krusa* and many a Swedish-American is still hampered by the custom.

It is not recorded in the Swedish chronicles who it was that first got the idea of mixing coffee with added stimulants. When cognac or *brännvin*—the native potato or grain aperitif, also called *akvavit*—is poured into the coffee in the cup, the drink is called a *kaffekask, kaffehalva,* or *kaffegök*. The latter appellation signifies the time of day the drink is taken, namely in the early morning before breakfast. It is supposed to serve as a protective measure against the insidious influence of the cuckoo bird's accented calling.

In earlier times another name for a mixed drink was *uddevallare*. This designation is said to have originated when sailors and fishmongers from the west coast, often from Uddevalla, brought coffee with them when visiting friends. On such occasions it was customary to treat them to a strong drink. It went into the coffee cup, making *uddevallare* all around. In some quarters this custom was not looked upon with favor, however, and at a parish meeting in Skåne in 1817 a notice was passed around forbidding the parishioners to partake of *uddevallare*.

At different times in Sweden coffee as such and strong drinks as well were forbidden for shorter or longer periods. The law prohibiting the use of coffee was finally abolished in 1822 and ever after coffee has been brewed and dripped and boiled to the heart's content of most Swedes. This is true with the exception of the war years when the import of coffee was stopped causing much stress, not to say anguish among coffee addicts. All kinds of substitutes were used. Even a concoction made from toasted dandelion roots had to be accepted as a tolerable drink. Was it any wonder that real coffee sent by anxious relatives and friends from this side of the world was so joyfully received!

For long years liquor was freely distilled at home— for household use, as it was designated. When in 1855 this home production (*husbehovsbränning*) was prohibited, a howling protest was heard all over the country, and it took a long time before the official arm of the law was able to reach and destroy the stills, ingeniously rigged up in homes of both high and low. A zealous clergyman, whose name was Peter Wieselgren (1800-1877), became widely known for his movement for total abstinence. He travelled from place to place and preached temperance with fury and fierceness. He unlashed his utter contempt for drunkenness in thundering sermons until the people winced. By the law of 1860 all manufacture of spirits was definitely restricted to government controlled plants, and farmers as well as city dwellers had to resort to these established places for their purchases.

In modern Sweden liquor sales were controlled by the so called Bratt System, which lasted for over forty years. Designed primarily for the purpose of stemming the abuse of strong drink, the famous—or infamous— passbook called *motbok* was introduced in Stockholm in 1914, and three years later it became a country-wide institution. It was the result of a careful investigation. A male passbook holder was permitted a maximum ration of three liters of hard liquor a month and an unmarried woman one liter. Wines were not prohibited. On the occasion of birthdays and other family events extra rations would be granted.

In restaurants a customer was allowed one glass of schnapps—but only in combination with food. As the waiter brought in the dish, the guest would smile slyly and ask: "Do I have to eat it?" More jokes have been told about the "rubber sandwich" that was carried in and then back to the kitchen, awaiting the next customer's glassy stare.

On October 1, 1955, the Bratt System was abolished. It was felt that the passbook had served its purpose. Liquor can now be bought in unlimited quantities. But with this new freedom new problems arise. Great efforts are made, for instance, to create a healthy attitude among young people in regard to drinking, if not advocating unconditional abstinence. A mild reminder to adult buyers of liquor is printed on the paper bags used by the government controlled stores. It says: *"En björntjänst att skaffa ungdomen sprit"* (a misguided service to furnish liquor to young people).

The Swedish regulations about drunken driving are rigorous. When going to a dinner party, a husband and wife will decide beforehand who is going to drive the car, and the spouse so willing abstains that evening from any alcoholic drinking—or they may choose to take a bus or taxi. They do not dare to take the chance of being stopped on the way home for a sobriety test. A prison term may await the guilty one and it is commonly known that neither a high position nor a titled name will safeguard the driver in such a situation.

As far as observation of ceremony goes, an abstaining guest at a dinner party need not feel left out. His wine glass will be filled as readily as those of the other guests, only that the drink is a nonalcoholic fruit punch instead of wine. And when the host proposes his welcome toast, all guests respond regardless of what is in their glasses.

The word *skål* has become internationally recognized and many interpretations have been suggested. It actually means bowl or vessel. In ancient times the mead or ale was poured in one large bowl and each guest helped himself by dipping the scoop, often made of wood and carved out in the shape of a bird, and drank out of it. And as the bird scoop went from hand to hand around the table and each guest drank out of it, he may have been saluted by the host in a phrase like *Ta för er ur skålen* (Help yourselves from the bowl). One may suggest that during an evening the host's prompting became a modified *skål* only and that this single word came to embrace all that was intended in the longer phrase. But whatever the Vikings had in mind, the custom today of extending a *skål* of welcome to a guest is truly an inherent part of Swedish hospitality.

**FROM STOVE TO TABLE**

# FROM STOVE TO TABLE

Is the Swedish housewife a good cook? An onrush of strong voices would answer an emphatic yes! And some would sing the praises of women from this province and that. Do not the women from Skåne know more about cooking than any other provincial practicer of the culinary arts? Others would maintain that the Småland women excel in preparing tasty dishes. Anyone who has eaten *ostkaka* (curd cake) can testify to that. And how about the women of Öland who have made *kroppkakor* their specialty? Inhabitants of Kalmar (the city opposite the island of Öland) still quibble with the islanders about the birthplace of this delicacy—and it is not yet settled. Translated literally the word means body cakes, and after having eaten a few one knows how they got the name. They are solid and bodybuilding! Here is the recipe:

Beat one egg and two egg yolks and blend with three cups of mashed potatoes. Beat in one heaped cup of flour, together with one teaspoon sugar, one and one-half teaspoon salt, and a pinch or two of pepper. Knead on a floured board and add more flour as needed for rolling out into a good half inch thick dough. Leave it for the moment and take four tablespoons minced salt pork, saute´ until tender, and season with a few sprinklings of ground cloves. Remove the pork from pan and saute´ two tablespoons minced onion in the fat. Mix the pork, onion, and three tablespoons cooked minced ham. Now cut the dough with a round cookie cutter and on half of the cakes put a teaspoon of the mixture. Place the rest of the cakes on top and press the edges together. Then roll the cakes into round balls. If there is more meat mixture left, make a hole in each ball and add. Then close the opening tightly. Drop the dumplings in salted, rapidly boiling water, one at a time, and let cook ten to twelve minutes. Turn them as they come floating to the top. If enough flour is used they will stay in shape. Serve at once with melted butter. The dumplings can be fried in deep fat instead of being boiled, or they can be baked and browned in the oven in a shallow buttered pan. Baste with butter! Any leftovers can be sliced the next day, fried, and served with lingonberries.

Food habits otherwise do not vary much from one part of Sweden to the other, with the exception of the coastal areas where fish is the mainstay. One thing is certain— the Swedish housewife has been busy at the art of cooking for centuries, with or without a cookbook. But when she dipped into *Cajsa Wargs Kokbok* she had a treasure house of recipes to choose from as well as hints in good housekeeping. Its official title was *Hjelpreda i hushållningen för unga fruentimber* (A Guide to Housekeeping for Young Women). In 1755, when it was published, the word *fruentimber* was proper and fitting, but today no young Swedish woman would like to be called *fruntimmer* (the present spelling). It sounds too old-fashioned. A new edition came out in 1946, which is a source of interesting information also to the housewife of today. The original author, Anna Christina Warg (1703-1769), did not always give the exact measurement, but said *"Man tager vad man haver,"* and *"Man tager om man så hava kan,"* which means—One takes what one has, and one takes (such and such an ingredient) if one has it handy. Today modern cookbooks crowd the Swedish book market, but the Warg cookbook still intrigues curious cooking experts, as do several other early recipe books. One such book, published in 1879 and considered a classic, is *Kokkonsten som veten-skap och konst* (The Art of Cooking as Science and Art). It was written by Charles Emil Hagdahl (1809-1897), an eminent physician of his time. His definition of a pinch is rather amusing. The Swedish language has two words for pinch—*pris* and *nypa*. Ordinarily they mean about the same, although when referred to snuff, the word *pris* is preferred—*en pris snus*. When referring to food, the good doctor maintained that *en pris* is the amount one takes between the thumb and forefinger and *en nypa* is what can be taken between the thumb, forefinger, and the middle finger.

One of the oldest (if not the very earliest Swedish cookbook) was brought out in modern setting in 1962. Anonymously published in 1650, it bore the title *Een lijten kockebook* (A Small Cookbook). The editor of the modern version, Per Erik Wahlund, calls it *En gammal svensk kokbok* (An Old Swedish Cookbook) and gives it a fond send-off in his introduction.

To the poorer class of Swedes there were times years back when not even a pinch of flour was left in the bin and salt herring and potatoes, alternating with porridge, called *gröt,* were the only food items on the table. Often the housewife, standing by the stove watching her family eat, was left without any food at all. It is no wonder that the Swedish emigrant on arrival in America marvelled at the abundance of food available to all. But he never forgot some of the eating habits from the old country. He still ate porridge. Bread and *gröt* remained the staff of life even after he was comfortably settled in new surroundings. For each time a new family moved into the community the neighbors brought a bowl of *flyttgröt,* made of rye meal, oat meal, or rice. It is an agelong Swedish custom to welcome those moving into new quarters with a bowl of porridge. Today it can take the form of a rice pudding, or any other kind of food suitable for the occasion. The sentiment is the same.

Another food custom introduced by the Swedes in this country is the popular *smörgåsbord,* literally a table with sandwiches. What it actually is can be described as an elaborate array of cold and hot food. One may wonder how the word originated. In an excerpt from Esaias Tegnér's essay on *smörgås,* written in 1894, the reference is made to a dissertation on the care of cattle in Norrland by Peter Wasenius. He tells that when churning butter on farms it was customary to shape the accumulated butter clusters into small balls, and so that an "eye" showed up on each one. Such a ball was called *smörgås* or *kärngås* from the verb *kärna* (to churn) and was served at the Saturday evening meal or on Sunday morning. Even to the smallest child, each member of the household was to have a taste.

But how did the round ball of butter (*smör*)become a *gås,* the Swedish word for goose? Could it be that the children standing around the churn watching identified the white clusters of butter in the milky liquid with what is called *vita gäss* (white geese), the name for the white foam riding the crest of a wave at sea? Generations of Swedish farm youth have seen the butter churn in action, and it is not too unlikely to assume that the small children made up their own idiom for the butter ball and that the expression came to be commonly accepted. It has also been suggested that *gås* comes from goose fat (*gåsister*) used by farming people as a spread on bread instead of butter.

There are other interpretations. By a flight of imagination, could it be possible that the skillful hands that manipulated the wooden spatulas in making butter balls, just by a touch and a swirl added a little beak to the round body? The eye was already there, supposedly. . . . And to the delight of the children a bird—a goose, if you will —would come into being—actually, a butter goose!

While the origin of *smörgås* is a matter for the etymologist to settle, the word *smörgåsbord* is part of everyone's vocabulary. It has become a concept in itself which brings to mind an elaborate and colorful display of different kinds of food, all decorated with sprigs of dill and parsley. And the butter balls continue to play a role in Swedish food habits, now appearing nicely grooved and stacked in a pyramid on the *smörgåsbord*. The meal is served buffet style, giving the guests a chance to feast their eyes in anticipation as they flock around the table. It begins with bread and butter, naturally, mostly dark breads and *knäckebröd* (hardtack), and seafood. *Sill* or herring is especially featured, appearing in many shapes and forms, and eaten with one or two small boiled potatoes. Having sampled the salty fare, a Swede likes at this moment a glass of ice cold *brännvin* or *akvavit* (water of life) as he sings the rousing *"Helan går . . ."* (bottoms up). A fresh plate from the stack and the meal begins in earnest. Leaving the cold cuts and the salads behind, the guests may now contemplate *småvarmt,* by which is meant appetizing tidbits from the stove. An omelet with mushrooms or asparagus is almost standard fare and often there is a dish especially catering to male taste called *"Janssons frestelse"* (Jansson's temptation)—whoever he was! Here is the recipe:

Take six medium size raw potatoes, peel and cut into thin narrow strips. Take ten to twelve anchovies, scrape them free from bones and cut into small pieces.

Butter and crumb a baking dish, alternate the layers
with potatoes and anchovies, and sprinkle chopped
onions and pepper between. The top layer should be
potatoes. Pour two cups of rich milk or cream over and
place a few dabs of butter on top. Bake in moderate
oven (375 F.) until the potatoes are done and the top
shows a delicate brown. This dish will be enough for
twelve servings for a *smörgåsbord* when small portions
are the rule.

It takes courage and a hardy stomach to continue the
meal with fish, meat, and dessert. At an elaborate dinner
party today the *smörgåsbord* is usually eliminated and
only a very small array of appetizers are served—in restaurants called *assietter*.

It would be wrong to think that the Swedes eat elaborate meals every day. They do not. Between *kalas* they
get along on such food as meatballs, *kåldolmar* (ground
meat wrapped in cabbage leaves), *pytt i panna,* which is
yesterday's leftovers of meat, cut and mixed with cubes of
boiled potatoes and onions—yes, hash. In the wintertime
on Thursdays the traditional food is *ärter och fläsk* (pea-
soup and boiled porkshanks) and *plättar och sylt* (small
pancakes and jam).

A few generations ago such plain food, in Swedish
called *husmanskost,* would have been regarded by some
Swedes a sumptuous repast. To them a meal meant merely
salt herring and potatoes, bread and gruel. They were the
rural laborers belonging to the proletarian class called
*statare* and *torpare,* who lived in unspeakable want and
poverty. Employed by a landed country squire, they
labored for a pittance and were housed in rickety, drafty
shacks divided into two or three family units. Usually big
flocks of children were milling about the place and from
the entrance ways their mothers would shout and scold,

despairing of ever having what they called *lugn och ro* (peace)!

Since 1945 such exploitation of man is by law forbidden, but to those having been involved the bitter memories linger. They feel cheated and begrudge not having had the opportunity to get ahead in life. There are exceptions, however. Although raised in such unfortunate circumstances, one group of intelligent individuals has succeeded in getting ahead. As writers they have gained names for themselves and in autobiographical novels they have made known the extent of their earlier privations. Their books have shocked readers with their detailed descriptions of life in a *statarstuga* (laborer's cabin). Many a Swedish emigrant could have added his own version. . . .

In his book *Godnatt, jord* (Goodnight, Earth), Ivar Lo-Johansson (1901- ) speaks in the racy, colorful language of his childhood, depicted as that of Mikael Bister. Instinctively Mikael was aware of a different mode of living, of a glowing life out there somewhere—if only he could reach it. His hunger for learning drove him to steal money in order to get books. Reflecting on it in another of his writings, the author claims he never had any pangs about the theft. "It was the fault of society."

How it felt to be wretchedly poor is sharply conveyed to the reader. There is no relief. Mikael is hopelessly immersed in a mire, unable to get out. As he grows older he contemplates on his life and that of his mother, father, and brother. Not many words were spoken between them. Silently his mother would stand by the stove preparing the scanty meals; in silence she would place the food on the table. Would there be enough to go around? Now and then she would sneak a glance at those at the table—there was never room for her to sit down. He would watch his mother's wrinkled face while the rest of the family was eating the water-soaked herring sprinkled with chives. Not until all had eaten did the mother approach the table. She would take her plate, place a few boiled potatoes on it, peel them, and then go over to the stove again, standing there while eating. It had always been like that. It was common practice. The men spread themselves out at the table but there was never any room for the women. They shied away like dogs who hurried off somewhere after having found a bone. All her life the mother had eaten while walking or sitting at the edge of the stove. Mikael Bister pondered about life around him and sometimes he felt as if fire burned inside. In those moments he did not know what to do with all that impelling force. In every direction the roads of escape seemed like narrow dark rat holes. Still he dreamed . . . some day he would have books, some day he would have enough to eat.

Poverty has been looked upon from many different angles, each one reflecting the view of the one who looked. The novelist Vilhelm Moberg (mentioned in connection with his emigrant books in the chapter "The Old Country") looks upon his childhood in a more detached, philosophical manner. As one of seven children living in a one room *stuga,* he was deprived of much of what is regarded as life's requisites, but still found it as it should be. In his autobiographical essay *"Brodd"* (Sprouting), he states his feelings of identity with the Småland countryside and his satisfaction of having been born in the country instead of in a crowded city.

Outside the confines of his home there was a free, clear view over the land. Nothing would hide the sun and the sky extended high above. Why was it always highest where he stood, he wondered. He felt a spontaneous joy in the change of seasons and looked at the drama of nature with curious eyes. Not until he began school did he become aware of the fact that all people did not live as they did at home. Some of his schoolmates brought more milk to school than they could drink, and one boy had a fried egg in his food bag every day. Could it be that people ate eggs every day without getting sick?

Aside from the limitation in food, Vilhelm Moberg's childhood was also conspicuous by its lack of books. He, too, suffered from *läshunger,* literally hunger for reading, and as he yearned for a book he even went into weeping spells in sheer despair. His family, completely unable to comprehend such agony, was quite worried and thought of consulting *en klok gumma,* an old woman wise in the mysteries of life and man. As he grew older and procured his first silver crowns, he sent for reading material from a loan library. The stipulation was that the books should circulate, but there was no one in his neighborhood to loan the books to!

An objective view on poverty is presented in Carl Jonas Love Almqvist's essay *"Svenska fattigdomens betydelse"* (The Meaning of Swedish Poverty). In his younger years this versatile author and poet (1793-1866) wrote by whim and fancy, but at the time he drafted the essay (in 1838) he had gained a more sober view of happenings around him. He looked at the common man with a new interest. To be poor is in part to reflect *nationlighet* (national characteristics), wrote the author. Of course, one must first have the knack, so to speak, of being poor and be able to resort to one's own resources. This God-given force within is the basic element of the Swedish national trait, he said. As the poverty-stricken man disengages himself from all worldly goods, he can stand free and feel God within and the whole world at his feet. Perhaps he looks ragged and dirty where he stands, but he can carry his head high and look around with eyes as if he lived everywhere instead of nowhere. This ability to fling all aside, to display a buoyant spirit in the face of misery, makes a Swede a Swede, says the author.

Did Carl Jonas Love Almqvist hit the core? While many a *statare* succumbed in spirit to poverty and merely endured life as it was measured out, a great many refused to believe that this was the kind of life God meant for them and their children. They stubbornly held to the God-given force within, believing there must be a way out. Some aspired and gained a crofter's holding, called *torp;* others packed up their belongings on a wagon and set out to work for some other *patron,* still hoping for a better living. A third way out was America, where there surely would be meat cooking on the stove and enough food on the table. And so tickets to America found their way to cottages around the land and the guarantee offered was a pair of strong arms and hands willing to work. By and by individuals as well as entire families would leave all behind for an unknown fate in the New World. These stouthearted Swedes—real Swedes according to Almqvist, who by the way also sought a new mode of living in America (1851) for other reasons than that of poverty—went forth with a firm determination to succeed. In most cases they did. And success meant good food to eat, and for the women the enjoyment of having enough ingredients available with which to prepare the dishes that they before only could visualize and long for. America had truly made cooking meaningful to the immigrant women and it put a lightness in their steps from stove to table.

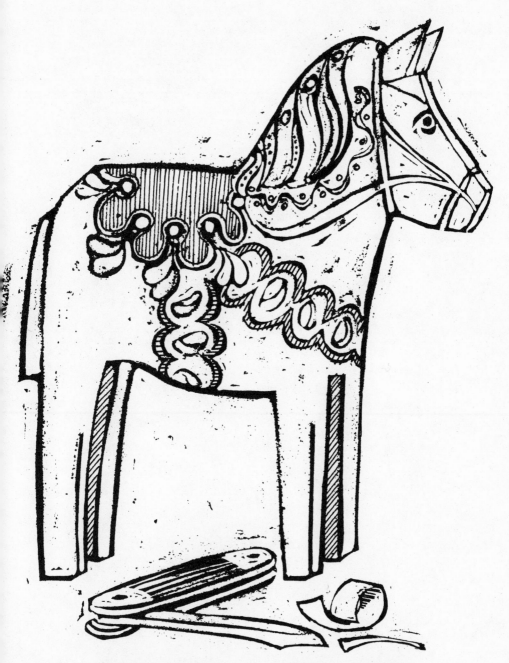

**HANDICRAFT IS TRADITIONAL**

# HANDICRAFT IS TRADITIONAL

In Sweden handicraft is a living tradition and it can be traced far back into bygone days. In the rural regions where the self-sufficient farm household utilized its own resources, handicraft and manual skills were cultivated out of necessity. Woolens were needed for clothing and bed covers and for the draperies covering the open side of built-in beds. Linens had to be woven to fill the need for towels, tablecloths, and bedsheets and the supply had to be ample considering the long periods between washings. So the loom kept the women occupied at all available hours while the men worked with wood, metal, and leather to produce sturdy, fine pieces of furniture, farm implements, and household items. Sometimes the needs exceeded what the family members could do themselves. In that event they employed professional craftsmen, who hired out their skills and traveled from farm to farm. It was an exciting day when any of these cobblers, tailors, carpenters, harness makers, or weavers arrived. Often they were quick-witted and just as often they carried interesting pieces of gossip from farms where they had stayed before. Their joining the family circle added color and spice to the sameness of everyday life.

In earlier times the Swedish country houses may have looked gray and insignificant on the outside, but the inside was rich in colors displayed in the weavings and in the painted furniture. These, together with hand-carved wooden spoons and platters, gaily decorated bowls, mugs, and crocks, and sturdy copper vessels, lent character to the room. The art form exemplified here, commonly called folk art, was governed by a quiet reserve and purposeful direction. It reflected conservatism in the sense that the creative expressions did not go beyond the acceptable for that particular region. Consequently, each province has come to embrace its own specialized product as something unique and different from the products of other parts of the country. For example, the gaily painted wooden toy horse is an item characteristic of Dalarna. Woven and embroidered wall hangings from Skåne have a pattern quite distinguishable in weave and color from that of other provinces. Hälsingland and Ångermanland produce linen weaves of an exceptionally high quality. From Gotland where sheep are plentiful came woolen bedcovers, wall hangings, pillow tops, and other pieces that are typical of the handiwork of this island.

The small town of Vadstena in Östergötland has for centuries been known for its handmade lace, dainty and feathery as a gossamer web. This art can be traced back to medieval times when nuns, skillful in lacemaking, came from the continent to Vadstena cloister and began teaching what in Swedish is called *knyppling* (done with bobbins, the threads being controlled with pins on a round padded board). The cloister was the center for the Birgittine order established in the name of Sweden's famous Saint Birgitta, who died in Rome in 1373, and was canonized eighteen years later. Through the centuries Vadstena carried the imprint of its monastic life and even today a small group of Birgittine nuns have established themselves there. Lacemaking continues to be an important artform among the townspeople. As a visitor to Vadstena strolls down the streets on a warm summer day, he may look into the gardens and discover one woman after another sitting under the trees twirling the bobbins with unbelievably swift and deft fingers, seemingly enjoying the out-of-doors while working.

Another form of handicraft is rug making. From north to south, Swedish homes have had handmade rugs on the floor since far back in time. *Trasmattor,* or rag rugs, were the most common. Following the strict rule that all things must be put to good use, the women of the family would gather up torn and worn clothing. Then, during the long winter evenings they would sit with their scissors and cut narrow strips of the cloth, sew them together, and roll them into large balls. When enough material was accumulated, they would weave yards and yards of carpet, measuring each length according to the size of the room. Another way of using the narrow strips was to braid them and sew them together into scatter rugs. *Trasmattor* are still the accepted floor covering in many Swedish homes today.

A more complicated technique is used in the handwoven runners made of cotton yarn in light colors, such as blue and white or red and white. This type of woven floor covering often appears in a decorative design of squares or geometric figures.

Rugs of truly imaginative, distinctive features are those produced by the *rya* technique. They are stitched in loops on a heavy piece of weaving with colorful wool yarn blended according to the given design. When cut, the loops make a deep soft pile. Formerly used as bed covers with the woolly nap turned under, these pieces offered great warmth. As their decorative value came to light, they became highly desirable floor coverings. Today the making of *ryamattor* is a very popular pastime and there is hardly

a home in Sweden that cannot boast such a rug, or where
there is not one under way. Men as well as women find
this kind of rug making intriguing. One of my male cousins
in Sweden, an engineer, makes one or two rugs each
winter and loves his work. So do his grown-up children,
because the rugs usually land in their homes!

Besides being a fascinating pastime, it has been ascer-
tained that *rya*-making is beneficial to the nerves. And
many an invalid, temporarily incapacitated, uses rug
making as therapy. It is felt that the handling of the soft,
colorful yarn and the tracing of the design is a wonderful
way to keep head and hands occupied during a conval-
escence.

Since Sweden is a country with an abundance of forests,
the material for wood carving is right at hand, and in
earlier days an amazing number of household items were
carved out of wood. During the long winter evenings the
men of the family made all kinds of useful articles, such
as bowls hollowed out of a piece of root, kegs, cheese
and butter molds, bins for flour and salt, boxes and
chests for storage, and special *kalasbyttor,* that is, vessels
for carrying prepared food to a wedding feast or to the
house of the bereaved. When invited to a funeral (you
still attend funerals in Sweden by invitation only) or a
wedding, both great occasions for eating, it was customary
that the guests bring dishes for the table. It was a matter
of pride to carry the food in an elaborately carved bowl
or box, and there was silent vying and viewing among
the guests to see how one's own vessel compared with the
others. If it did not make a visible impression, one can
theorize that the men of the family were ordered to produce something more elaborate for the next occasion.

Each guest brought his own knife and spoon, which
were usually beautifully carved. Often such table items

were given to a bride as a betrothal gift and they were used and treasured by her throughout her lifetime. The fork came in use rather late among the people on the farms.

Drinking cups were also carved out of wood, sometimes in the shape of a hollowed out bird, the beak or tail being used as a handle. Other drinking containers included bowls with four nibs and large scooped out vessels with elaborately carved handles. Beer mugs were often colorfully painted.

Baskets were important household items and a well equipped farm home had a good supply of them. They were made from roots, twigs, fibre, or straw and had many practical uses. Small baskets and boxes were often made of birch bark and many are the homes in America where grandfather's snuff box is still kept and treasured.

What is produced and sold in Sweden today in the line of handicraft goes under the name *hemslöjd*. The genuineness of the products is guaranteed by the round cardboard tag attached to each article, carrying the above word or the two words *Svensk slöjd,* meaning Swedish homecraft. The artistic standard is maintained by the local homecraft societies, of which there are about forty in Sweden today, and the national association in Stockholm. The societies aid the home worker in selecting the right kind of yarn, material, or artistic blends of colors. These same organizations also arrange courses in weaving and other handicrafts and frequently furnish samples for country fairs and exhibits.

This organized aim and design to cultivate the innate talent and artistic bent of the Swedish people came about as a desperate attempt to stem, as far as homecraft is concerned, the process of the nineteenth century industrialism, which caused the dulling of artistic taste and a turning away from the time-honored traditions to a prefer-

ence for machine-made goods. The old cupboard, carved
and painted by grandfather, was discarded for a fancy
machine-made piece of furniture. The old bench cushions
and wall hangings were put away and replaced with fabric
of less body and less durability. It was more exciting to
go to the village store and select some printed calico for a
dress than to sit for long hours and weave so many yards
of heavy, unyielding material. The sense for the genuine,
traditional product deteriorated and was almost lost when
the great guardian of Sweden's primitive art, Artur Hazelius
(1833-1901), began his life work to save and to revive
the old crafts. He traveled about, talking with people,
encouraging them to reappraise the art and ancient values
of their forefathers. He established weaving schools and
collected old colorful samples in weaving technique. This
pioneer, so fired with his idea, succeeded in saving a great
deal of the traditional primitive art and interested others in
his work. The idea grew into a movement. In Dalarna, for
instance, where traditions are deep-rooted, leading artists
of the time (Carl Larsson at Sundborn, Anders Zorn in
Mora, Gustaf Ankarcrona at Holen) became instrumental
in a concerted drive for the preservation of old articles,
such as painted wall hangings, weavings, copper vessels,
hand-tooled furniture, parish costumes, prepared sheep-
skins, and leather goods.

Eventually, the museum in Stockholm called Nordiska
Museet came to house what is now a unique, magnificent
collection of old furniture, weavings, and costumes from
bygone days. Within the wide expanse of Skansen, the
open-air ethnographical museum located nearby, old cottages and farm buildings from different parts of Sweden
were moved into wooded areas resembling the original
surroundings. Today these buildings number about one
hundred twenty, including the house where Artur Hazelius

was born. A visitor can now spend a greatly rewarding day at Skansen, strolling from cabin to cabin and viewing its interior as it was in earlier times. Following the winding paths through the woods, he can take a look at the animal life at the zoo, he can watch folk dancers perform in their native costumes to the rhythmic beat of fiddle and accordion, or dance himself at the dance pavilion provided for the public. He can watch glass-blowing and see how a beautiful vase is created, or visit the old apothecary shop, or pay a call at the manor house Skogaholm, moved here from the province of Närke. He can listen to an evening's concert, stop for coffee and waffles at the open-air cafe, or dine at the restaurant Solliden, whatever suits him best. No doubt he will take a look at Seglora church, brought here from Västergötland, where marriage ceremonies often are performed. In short, Skansen provides a number of services as well as entertainment, and in the summertime it is a popular gathering place for Stockholmers and tourists alike.

So far the primitive art. What characterizes Swedish art of today? So much has been written on Swedish Modern that it is difficult to sum up the total in a few words. To counteract with questions, is it not an expression of elegant simplicity? Is it not a unique blending of agelong ideals and finely balanced modernism? Does it not express the artist's innate love of form and flowing lines? Though contemporary design is modern in every sense of the word, it is strongly rooted in the past. The victory of industrialism brought about a new way of life, but the original artistic values could not be suppressed. The intrinsic nature of this tradition is a feeling, an awareness of the art developed through centuries, and it is reflected in the desire to embrace the genuine, the real, the time-honored. The craftsman's loving, sensitive use of his material, be it wood, steel, glass, wool, linen, or whatever, results in unique, artistically executed objects of form-true style. The textiles and upholstery fabrics of today show varied, striking patterns reflecting the high artistic standard which is formed and maintained through a close cooperation between artist, designer, and industrial producer.

Although a young Swedish couple of today will have a modern streamlined home, the love of traditional values comes to light in the way an old chair, a chest, or a cupboard is treasured. Such choice pieces were built to last and they carry all the earmarks of skill and fine craftsmanship. In textiles, glass, ceramics, and utilitarian items, however, the choice is the latest design. And the present happy union of art and industry is producing household articles with a well-proportioned elegance. Swedish Modern is functional and beautifully designed, thereby earning the contemporary slogan, *vackrare vardagsvara,* which conveys the constant striving for "added beauty in things for everyday use."

**MYTHS AND LEGENDS**

## MYTHS AND LEGENDS

Swedish people of today are fondly tolerant of old concepts and beliefs. But in earlier days superstition or *skrock* ruled the way of life and the belief in *troll,* gnomes, elfs, and fairies was firmly rooted. It was accepted without question and transmitted from generation to generation, until in later years popular enlightenment effaced the practice. Or did it? We are all guilty of some manifestation of it. A Swede is apprehensive when a black cat rushes across the road in front of his car and between his teeth he hisses: "Twee, twee, twee!" He throws a pair of old shoes, playfully to be sure, after some one who is embarking on an important venture, or simulates a kick in the back in order to ensure success in the undertaking. He shrinks at the idea of thirteen at the table. Many, many more are the superstitions that tenaciously hold out to this day.In something as truly modern as Orrefors glassware, traditional observance is depicted. In one of their popular vases the motif is a little girl who stands pinching her wide skirt as she supposedly curtsies to the new moon on the opposite wall of the vase. In curtsying three times she would get her wish fulfilled, according to legend.

At New Year's it was a favorite pastime in some parts of Sweden to watch for the new moon, and with meat and bread and a hymnbook in his hand, the farmer would wish for a prosperous year. After bowing three times, he would open the hymnbook at random and read the lines that caught his eyes. With his own interpretation of the words he would have a good year—or bad, as the words went. The moon, aside from its romantic influence, was said to cast a dangerous spell on anyone who would expose himself to its rays for any length of time, as in sleep, for instance. They would cause *månstyng,* affecting the mind, it was told. They would even make a knife lose its biting edge.

*Troll* is one of several Swedish words that baffle the translator. Although the English language has adopted the word *troll* from the Scandinavians with approximately the same meaning—a supernatural creature of ugly mien and stature—the Swede has definitely read a bit more into it. A Swede might say about a person who defies the rules of decency—*Han bär sig åt som ett riktigt troll* (He behaves like a regular *troll*). The Swedish concept depends on the impression from childhood reading of fairy tales. There we read of the gruesome experiences of human beings when encountering *troll* and how the belief in their evil power influenced the fate of man. To invoke the name of God was a sure means of protection, however, which comes to light in the poem *"Den lilla kolargossen"* (The Charcoal Burner's Son) by Erik Gustaf Geijer (1783-1847). A little boy who is frightened to death of *troll* is running through the forest to the charcoal kiln where his father works, and sinking down exhausted at his side, he is greeted by the reassuring words: "Den rätt kan läsa sitt Fader vår, han rädes varken fan eller trollen, fast det är mörkt, långt, långt bort i skogen." (He who properly can read the Lord's Prayer is neither afraid of devil nor *troll,* although it is dark far, far away in the forest.)

It cannot be said that anyone has ever seen a *troll,* and yet, in the concept of people of old they had shape and form. They had a tail, and they were ugly to look at, because they had a hideous face with drooping jowls and warty noses, and hair that seemed like a tangled mass of straw. That *troll* sometimes were invisible to man was due to their fear of man. When approached by a human being, they would often take the shape of a scraggly log, a boulder, or even a mountain. They lived under the roots of trees, or in caves and hollows, and there they gathered their loot of silver and gold, stolen from human beings. The story goes that many a man who tried to find the treasure house of *troll* was captured and dragged into the cave, never to be seen again. It is also told that many a young maiden was lured into the hall of the mountain king (*bergakungen*). He lived in lofty, palatial rooms glittering and alluring to the curious one looking in, but a prison as the doors slammed shut behind her. In the case of a princess so captured, her father would offer half his kingdom and the hand of his daughter to any man who could rescue her. Princes, knights, and warriors, brave and handsome, would search for her, but in vain. Comes a poor farm lad, afraid neither of *troll* nor dark caves, and by artful cunning he succeeds in finding and rescuing the young princess, and the two would live happily ever after.

The common *troll* was said to confine his lust for humans to children. It was believed that *troll* mothers would try to exchange their own ugly offspring for a human child and by magic prevail on the parents to accept the *troll* youngster as their own. But sooner or later it would give away its true identity and the *troll* mother would be forced to return the real child. The reason a human child could play with *troll* children without harm was that a *troll* has no power over a human who is unafraid. Children did not have the sense to be afraid! In any situation with a *troll,* the ringing of church bells would at once release his hold on a human being.

The belief in a personified devil or *fan* (pronounced fahn) was prevalent for centuries, and only by the word of God or the sign of the cross could his wicked attempts to lead humans astray be averted. *Fan* is a commonly used word of imprecation in Sweden and is not spoken vainly. When the word began to appear in letters from America in connections not making good sense, the confusion and concern among the home folks in Sweden were considerable. What could Oskar mean by writing that he could not sleep in the hot summer nights without having "fan" at his side? What kind of country was America, anyway?

Otherwise the name for the devil is *djävulen,* or *den onde, hin håle, satan,* just to mention a few. From Luther's catechism the passage *djävulen, världen och vårt eget kött* (the devil, the world, and our own flesh) is remembered by most Swedes from childhood days. It had to be learned by heart in its entirety and when being spoken with punctuated emphasis from the pulpit, the words made a deep impression. Today, Swedish children are not requested to learn such passages by heart, at least not until the words are understood. Also, in Swedish-American communities there were zealous clergymen who preached with conviction and warned their congregations of the devil's power. An American woman of Swedish descent told of her childhood impression of a sermon: "My father who was a minister and preached in Swedish had a booming voice, and, being a big man, he looked imposing when he stood in the pulpit. I can remember how frightened I was when his fierce words rang out over the congregation. One occasion stands out vividly in my mind. Raising his arm and pointing upwards he thundered: 'Gud vakar! Men djävulen vakar också!' (God watches! But the devil watches, too!) Not until I grew up did I learn what the words meant, but they were etched in my mind all those years. They meant that both God and the devil watch."

The commonly accepted image of a personified devil, frightful in appearance, also included his fire-brimmed habitation, *helvetet* or hell. Many an artist has depicted imaginary scenes from hell, showing tortured beings in one mass of twisted bodies, all enveloped in flames. From childhood this writer has vivid recollections of such paintings in the ceiling of Hakarp church in Småland, and how awesome but fascinating it was to look at them. Not even a stern rebuke from mother could stem the curiosity and the urge to look just once more at those terrifying pictures.

By universal folk tradition the devil is fiercely made and his apparition grisly to behold. In the *Devil's Bible,* which can be seen at the Royal Library in Stockholm, he is depicted as gruesome as the beholder saw him, and the story of this creative work reads like a legend—which it is! The book, almost a yard in height, has been considered one of the world's seven wonders.

The Library gives the following account:

"The Codex Gigas (Giant Book) or Devil's Bible contains the Old and the New Testaments in pre-Vulgate Latin translations. The manuscript was written in the early thirteenth century in the Benedictine Monastery of Pod-lazic in Bohemia, the vellum used having been prepared from the skins of one hundred and sixty asses. It is called the Devil's Bible after the impressive picture of that potentate on the folio shown here. According to legend the scribe was a monk who had been confined to his cell for some breach of monastic discipline, and who, by way of penance, finished the manuscript in one single night with the help of the devil whom he had summoned to help him. In 1594 the manuscript was acquired by the Imperial Treasury in Prague. When the Swedish Army conquered the city in 1648 it was brought to Sweden and presented to the Royal Library the following year."

The surest way to free a human being from the evil powers of the devil was to speak out words from the Holy Writ in a loud voice. The devil would also shrink away at the sight of the cross. And the *ellakors* (elf's cross), a special kind of pendant, was a never-failing protection against evil powers, even sickness. But it had to be made from nine different pieces of inherited silver and when calling for it at the silversmith's, no word should be spoken. If this happened the magic spell was broken.

When a Swede is bent on using strong language, he might for the sake of euphony resort to the word *fanders*, or other words derived from *fan*. In such an old expression as *dra åt häklefjäll* he states a desire to dispatch his fellowman to place far removed. Iceland with its mountain Hekla is not very near and serves the purpose. Incidentally, the word *fjäll* stands for a snowcapped mountain. High places were the favorite gathering spots for witches and evil spirits, so says the legend, and woe unto the human being who was out in the field when they came riding on their broomsticks through the murky skies on the way to a tryst with the devil. The fictitious mountain Blåkulla was supposed to be such a meeting place, and it was especially at Easter time and on Walpurgis night, April 30, that they were astir to carry out their malevolent conjurations.

Other supernatural beings were the benevolent fairies, although there were ugly fairies among them who sometimes conjured forth disagreeable situations for newborn infants. Others wafted their magic wands to confer happiness on a favored human being. No one could determine the whereabouts of these creatures. However, when the evening mist swept across the meadows, a lone wanderer might see them flitting about. In his poem "Näcken" (The Nix), Erik Johan Stagnelius (1793-1823) depicts the scene with these beautiful lines: "Kvällens guldmoln fästet kransa, älvorna på ängen dansa, och den bladbekrönta Näcken gigan rör i silverbäcken." And in prose translation—The golden clouds of evening encircle the sky; the elves are dancing in the meadow and the leaf-crowned water sprite plays in the silvery brook.

Carl von Linne,́ the illustrious botanist, traveled at one time on the island of Öland, located on Sweden's east coast, and made an interesting observation about the fairy-dancing. Yes, the fairies had been seen below the rampart, but when he came to examine the phenomenon more closely he discovered a creeping grass with blue leaves that grows into a round swirl. He realized that "foolish" people, looking at this blue mist of growth from a distance, might imagine seeing fairies dancing!

*Näcken, Bäckahästen, Strömkarlen, Forskarlen* are all water sprites dwelling in lakes, streams, and waterfalls. Sadness seems to be their lot because of their failure to obtain release from the unwanted incarceration. Such a release could only come about through contact with a human being, and many were the tricks used to lure a young maiden to their side. From the waterfall late at night people would hear *Strömkarlen* play his fiddle, and sad and wailing were the tunes coming from his strings. *Strömkarlen* has been portrayed by the sensitive artist Ernst Josephson (1851-1906) as his imagination saw him, and this painting has become a symbol of longing for the unattainable. It is exhibited in the collections of the late Prince Eugen at Valdemarsudde, Stockholm, which became a museum after the death of the prince in 1947.

Another version of the painting belongs to Göteborg's Museum of Art.

*Maran,* the personification of nightmare, is supposed to look like a human being during the day, but at night takes on the disguise of a gruesome phantom, impelled to torture man and beast. Another disguise was that of a wolf, who had a tricky way of appearing like a normal ordinary neighbor but at midnight changed into the frightening disguise of a wolf. By common belief he was cursed by some one and could not be released until part of his clothing was brought to church and blessed.

Another dangerous being lurking about was the wood nymph called *skogsrå,* and a man walking through the forest should look out. She was supposed to have a beautiful face and body, but her back was hollowed out and empty. She could appear in other places than the forest, even in the city. It was in Karlstad, Värmland, that the inventor Kevenhüller in Selma Lagerlöf's famous story, *Gösta Berlings Saga,* encountered the wood nymph. He was dazzled by her appearance. Dressed in shimmering green silk, she was the most beautiful woman he had ever seen. Enchanted, he looked into her shiny green eyes and admired the abundance of blond hair that reached almost to the ground. He was not unaware, however, of the pine needles and fern leaves nestled in it. A cloak over her shoulders covered her back, but underneath Kevenhüller caught sight of the tail dragging behind. He bowed low. "Would it please your grace to pick up the train?" He could not bear to have her the laughing-stock of all the city people. In appreciation of his polite, kind ways, the wood nymph bestowed on him the gift of inventive power, provided that only one copy of each invention was made. Kevenhüller became famous. He made a carriage that went by itself uphill and downhill; he made a stone tower of great strength and beauty like a knight's fort with a windmill's sails on it. He made a fire wheel that whirled around sending out sparks in all directions. Being a genius had not made him happy, however, and finally he implored the wood nymph to release him, and make him an ordinary man again. And she did. Such is the power of a wood nymph!

Many older Swedish people have gruesome tales to tell about *spöken* or spooks, and even if they themselves never have seen a ghost, their grandparents surely had had that experience. They would tell that the dead have been known to *gå igen,* that is, reappear after death. Almost every castle in Sweden is said to harbor a ghost, often called *vita frun* or the lady in white, who by folk tradition roams the palace halls at night in search of something, or stands by the window on a moonlit night wringing her hands. The assumption is that a tragic phase of her life had gone unsolved and that her spirit cannot rest until the wrong has been rectified. Her appearance augurs no good, as is revealed in the poem *"Vita frun"* by Carl Snoilsky (1841-1903). Jesper, the palace guard, trembles in his boots as he watches the white ghost at the window, clearly outlined in the bright moon light. She gropes and fumbles with her hands as if washing a cloth. He is terrified and drops his spear. At that moment the cock crows—and the lady in white vanishes out of sight. Bad times are approaching. . . .

Does modern man believe in ghosts? The practically minded Swede of today is apt to smile indulgently at such a suggestion and explain away any weird experience that comes to his attention. The mind plays tricks, he says. Still, the subject can come up and be discussed with lively, curious interest whenever the mood and atmosphere are right for story-telling, and there is hardly anyone who has not a grandmother or aunt who has not experienced the weirdest happenings, the telling of which makes one's hair stand on end. So the subject of ghosts and spooks continues to intrigue the minds of men, and attempts at finding acceptable answers to supernatural occurrences are noteworthy. But the inscrutable, enigmatical "something" which today is apt to be explained away by logic and scientific clarifications was in earlier days accepted as part of the course of life. After having seen his father's ghost, Hamlet states: "There are more things in heaven and earth, Horatio, than are dreamt of in your philosophy."

The magic power of good was exemplified by *tomten* (the brownie) who lived under the farm house and watched out for danger of fire and other hazards, and guarded man and beast in general. All the year around he was busy tending sick cattle and always notifying the farmer by a nudge when danger was afoot. He was the last one to retire at night to make sure that all doors were locked and that the lamps and candles were turned out. He was a coveted creature to have around, and concern was expressed that he would find everything to his liking so he would stay on. He did not like arguments and harsh words, and with a pounding on the wall he would make his people aware of it.

Even city people are conscious of *tomten*. When they build a small cottage for the summer, they are prone to call it Tomtebo or Tomteborg, making facetious remarks about having invited *tomten* to dwell on their property, so that all will go well. And *tomten* is so easy to have. All he asks is a plate of *risgrynsgröt* (rice porridge) on Christmas Eve. No one has ever been able to report, however, if he is enjoying his fare, but strangely enough it is generally gone when morning comes.

"How tall is a *tomte*?" This question was put to the

writer at Christmas time one year by a woman who was going to speak at her club about Swedish traditions. When she was told that no one can ascertain the height of such an imaginary creature, she was visibly disappointed and blurted out: "So . . . you haven't seen one?"

In the opening chapter of Selma Lagerlöf's *The Wonderful Adventures of Nils,* a *tomte* appears before the unbelieving eyes of a fourteen-year-old boy. What first seemed a shadow became clear and Nils actually saw *tomten* sitting on the edge of the chest, it says. Of course, he had heard of *tomtar,* but he never dreamt that they could be that small. Because what he saw was a tiny little man not taller than a hand's breadth. He was old and wrinkled and had no beard. He was dressed in a black frock coat, knee breeches, and a black broad-brimmed hat. He was very neat and trim with white lace about his throat and around his wrists. He had buckles on his shoes and garters tied in bows.

This description differs from the one generally conceived of and resembles more that of a sprite or an imp. An "ordinary" *tomte* is short, to be sure, but supposedly of man size. In her short story *Tomten på Töreby* from *Troll och människor* (Trolls and Men) Selma Lagerlöf depicts *tomten* this way: "He was small and gray and dressed in knee breeches and gray jacket with silver buttons." She calls him *Gamlefar.*

In the story *Viggos Adventure on Christmas Eve"* by the poet and scholar in the field of cultural history and religion, Viktor Rydberg (1828-1895), *tomten* or *julvätten* as he is called here, is depicted as a small old man with a face full of wrinkles and a beard similar to the moss on the roof of a cottage. His clothes are rough and shaggy from top to toe. Out of the corner of his mouth hangs a pipe.

The illustrator for this story was Jenny Nyström, a name that has ever since been closely associated in the consciousness of the Swedish people with bearded *tomtar*. It is told that the author was so pleased with the way she had portrayed his *tomte* that he actually considered the pictures soothing to the nerves, even tranquilizing! Soon Jenny Nyström's *tomtar* appeared in other publications, especially in Christmas magazines and on Christmas cards, and it can be said that at the beginning of the 1890's *jultomten* had stepped out of a gray, misty past and taken shape and color, red stocking cap and all. To the generation that grew up from that time there could be no other representation, it seemed. And attempts to modernize the little fellow have met with disapproval.

To a middle-aged couple in Stockholm, Jenny Nyström's *"Jultomten"* was worth 875 crowns (approximately $175.00), as they bid and purchased this water color painting at an art collector's auction in the fall of 1961. Besides being the creator of the concept of *jultomten*, Jenny Nyström gave an enduring character to the living conditions of her time.

Was *tomten* always good? In most cases he is portrayed as the benevolent fellow who is helpful and patient too, as is told in the story of Viggo. From his chest in the sleigh the visiting *jultomte* distributed gifts to the people as he rode from farm to farm, but first asked the *hustomte* (the little fellow dwelling on the farm) what kind of people he watched over. When told that they were wicked and mean the visitor said: "Try to stay for another year, otherwise peace and harmony will disappear from this farm."

There is another side to *tomten*, however, and situations have occurred when he used the rod. As a representative of conscience, he appeared the moral guardian. Nils Holgerson received a stinging blow on his ear when he willfully tried to keep the small sprite down in the fly net. The master of Töreby was tricked into submission—and death —because *Gamlefar* was not satisfied with the way he managed his estate. And one reads in the old tales how the milkpail sometimes was knocked down without visible reason, and that the sound of striking hammers was heard under the house. Then the farmer knew that *tomten* was peeved about something and realized that he had better set things right.

The fondly accepted image of *tomten* created by hearsay, tales, and legends has in modern times been firmly established by Viktor Rydberg's cherished poem, entitled *"Tomten."*

### TOMTEN

Midvinternattens köld är hård,
stjärnorna gnistra och glimma.
Alla sova i enslig gård
djupt under midnattstimma.
Månen vandrar sin tysta ban,
snön lyser vit på fur och gran,
snön lyser vit på taken.
Endast tomten är vaken.

Står där så grå vid ladgårdsdörr,
grå mot den vita driva,
tittar som många vintrar förr,
upp emot månens skiva,
tittar mot skogen, där gran och fur
drar kring gården sin dunkla mur,
grubblar, fast ej det lär båta,
över en underlig gåta.

För sin hand genom skägg och hår,
skakar huvud och hätta—
"nej, den gåtan är alltför svår,
nej, jag gissar ej detta"—
slår, som han plägar, inom kort
slika spörjande tankar bort
går att ordna och pyssla,
går att sköta sin syssla.

Går till visthus och redskapshus,
känner på alla låsen—
korna drömma vid månens ljus
sommardrömmar i båsen;
glömsk av sele och pisk och töm
Pålle i stallet har ock en dröm:
krubban han lutar över
fylls av doftande klöver;—

Går till stängslet för lamm och får,
ser, hur de sova där inne;
går till hönsen, där tuppen står
stolt på sin högsta pinne;
Karo i hundbots halm mår gott,
vaknar och viftar svansen smått,
Karo sin tomte känner,
de äro goda vänner.

Tomten smyger sig sist att se
husbondfolket det kära,
länge och väl han märkt att de
hålla hans flit i ära;
barnens kammar han sen på tå
nalkas att se de söta små,
ingen må det förtycka:
det är hans största lycka.

Så har han sett dem, far och son,
ren genom många leder
slumra som barn; men varifrån
kommo de väl hit neder?
Släkte följde på släkte snart,
blomstrade, åldrades, gick—men vart?
Gåtan, som icke låter
gissa sig, kom så åter!

Tomten vandrar till ladans loft:
där har han bo och fäste
högt på skullen i höets doft,
nära vid svalans näste;
nu är väl svalans boning tom,
men till våren med blad och blom
kommer hon nog tillbaka,
följd av sin näpna maka.

Då har hon alltid att kvittra om
månget ett färdeminne,
intet likväl om gåtan, som
rör sig i tomtens sinne.
Genom en springa i ladans vägg
lyser månen på gubbens skägg,
strimman på skägget blänker,
tomten grubblar och tänker.

Tyst är skogen och nejden all,
livet där ute är fruset,
blott från fjärran av forsens fall
höres helt sakta bruset.
Tomten lyssnar och, halvt i dröm,
tycker sig höra tidens ström,
undrar, varthän den skall fara,
undrar, var källan må vara.

Midvinternattens köld är hård,
stjärnorna gnistra och glimma.
Alla sova i enslig gård
gott intill morgontimma.
Månen sänker sin tysta ban,
snön lyser vit på fur och gran,
snön lyster vit på taken.
Endast tomten är vaken.

### THE HOUSE-GOBLIN

Cold is the night, and still, and strange,
Stars they glitter and shimmer.
All are asleep in the lonely grange
Under the midnight's glimmer.
On glides the moon in gulfs profound;
Snow on the firs and pines around,
Snow on the roofs is gleaming.
All but the goblin are dreaming.

Gray he stands at the barnyard door,
Gray by the drifts of white there,
Looks, as oft he has looked before,
Up at the moon so bright there;
Looks at the woods, where the fir-trees tall
Shut the grange in with their dusky wall;
Ponders—some problem vexes,
Some strange riddle perplexes—

Passes his hand o'er beard and hair,
Shaking his head and cap then:
"Nay, that riddle's too hard, I swear,
I'll ne'er guess it mayhap then."
But, as his wont is, he soon drives out
All such thoughts of disturbing doubt,
Frees his old head of dizziness,
And turns him at once to business.

First he tries if the locks are tight,
Safe against every danger.
Each cow dreams in the pale moonlight
Summer dreams by her manger.
Dobbin, forgetful of bits that gall,
Dreams like the cows in his well-filled stall,
Leaning his neck far over
Armfuls of fragrant clover.

Then through the bars he sees the sheep,
Watches how well they slumber,
Eyes the cock on his perch asleep,
Round him hens without number.
Carlo wakes at the goblin's tread,
Wags then his tail and lifts his head;
Well acquainted the two are,
Friends that both tried and true are.

Last the goblin slips in to see
How all the folk are faring.
Long have they known how faithfully
He for their weal is caring.
Treading lightly on stealthy toes,
Into the children's room he goes,
Looks at each tiny treasure:
That is his greatest pleasure.

So he has seen them, sire and son,
Year by year in that room there
Sleep first as children every one.
Ah, but whence did they come there?
This generation to that was heir,
Blossomed, grew old, and was gone—but where?
That is the hopeless, burning
Riddle ever returning.

Back to the barn he goes to rest,
Where he has fixed his dwelling
Up in the loft near the swallow's nest,
Sweet there the hay is smelling,
Empty the swallow's nest is now,
Back though he'll come when the grass and bough
Bud in the warm spring weather,
He and his mate together.

Always they twitter away about
Places through which they've travelled,
Caring naught for the goblin's doubt,
Though it were ne'er unravelled.
Through a chink in one of the walls
Moonlight on the old goblin falls,
White o'er his beard it wanders;
Still he puzzles and ponders.

Forest and field are silent all,
Frost their whole life congealing,
Save that the roar of the waterfall
Faintly from far is stealing.
Then the goblin, half in a dream,
Thinks it is Time's unpausing stream,
Wonders wither 't is going,
And from what spring 't is flowing.

Cold is the night, and still, and strange,
Stars they glitter and shimmer.
All yet sleep in the lonely grange
Soundly till morn shall glimmer.
Now sinks the moon in night profound;
Snow on the firs and pines around,

Snow on the roofs is gleaming.
All but the goblin is dreaming.

Translated by **Charles Wharton Stork**
*Anthology of Swedish Lyrics*
The American-Scandinavian Foundation, New York
London: Humphrey Milford
Oxford University Press, 1930

OUT OF DEEP WELLS

## OUT OF DEEP WELLS . . .

From the Proverbs of the Old Testament to the proverbs emanating from the contributions of many cultures, the collective wisdom of the ages became a rich well out of which the world at large may still draw. By a common concept these proverbs became words of magic. Originating from the mouths of kings and prophets they carried weight, and when found applicable to every day life they transmuted into popular bywords. Introduced in Latin by monks, minstrels, and troubadours, they were fashioned into other languages and in time absorbed. That is, if the translation succeeded in bringing out a witty turn of phrase. If not, the proverb would fall into oblivion.

Comparing proverbs with other aspects of folklore, such as tales, anecdotes, narratives, ballads, and folk songs, they are short, tersely cogent, and render that which is true in a few pithy words. The early Northmen used sayings from *Havamal,* which were succinct adages from ancient Scandinavian history reflecting Viking traditions.

In Sweden today proverbs are often fitted into conversations and letters and public utterances. A Minnesota student, proud of his knowledge of Swedish, was at one time present at the Sweden-America Day held at Skansen, Stockholm, each summer. He was asked to "say a few words" to the thousands of people who had gathered there, and as he told it later he faltered and quavered and failed

to get the Swedish words out in proper order. Then, in a
flash, he recalled a proverb he had learned in a Swedish
class at the University, and as he regained his confidence
he grinned and explained that as long as his head felt so
empty he had better not say anything more but to conclude with the telling proverb, *Tomma tunnor skramla
mest,* which means: Empty barrels make the loudest noise.
He was much applauded.

Swedish proverbs cover many subjects. Often they
reveal concepts of man's attitude towards God, who is
referred to as *Vår Herre,* or Our Lord. These proverbs
reflect the image of a close personal relationship with
God as the Father who manages human affairs in accord-
ance with man's merit. This image can be traced throughout folk tradition. In the folk art of Dalarna, for instance,
he was depicted as an elderly gentleman dressed in a
native frock coat and high silk hat as he walked the earth
advising and blessing his people.

The following proverbs exemplify the above theme:

Döden är Vår Herres sopkvast
Death is our Lord's broom

Allt har en början utom Vår Herre
Everything has a beginning except our Lord

Vår Herre är bra att ha när åskan går
It is good to have our Lord when it thunders

Med Vår Herre är man ömsom vän och ömsom ovän
One is either friend of our Lord or an enemy

När Vår Herre ger ska man hålla säcken öppen
When our Lord gives one should keep the sack open

Den som står väl hos Vår Herre kan höra gräset gro
He who has the good will of our Lord can hear the
grass grow

Here follows a listing of proverbs of a general nature:

1. Lagom är bäst
2. Högmod går före fall
3. Bränt barn skyr elden
4. Otack är världens lön
5. Nya kvastar sopa bäst
6. Tillfället gör tjuven
7. Av skadan blir man vis
8. Egen härd är guld värd
9. Små grytor ha också öron
10. Borta bra, men hemma bäst
11. Den illa gör han illa far
12. En svala gör ingen sommar
13. Som man bäddar får man ligga
14. Man får ta seden dit man kommer
15. Man ska inte kasta pärlor för svin
16. Vad som göms i snö kommer upp i tö
17. Man ska smida medan järnet är varmt
18. När katten är borta dansa råttorna på bordet
19. Små barn, små bekymmer—stora barn, stora bekymmer
20. När det regnar välling har den fattige ingen sked

These old proverbs are a telling part of Swedish culture and many Swedish-Americans have no doubt heard some of them since childhood. To offer a translation would be a disservice, would it not? Let these sayings be a challenge to memory and to the knack of interpretation! If, on the other hand, a reader of non-Swedish background should be gripped by curiosity as to what it all means, a translation can be found at the back of the book!

Our times gather words of wisdom, too. Collected under the name aphorisms, they differ from proverbs in the respect that they are not anonymous. Magnus von Platen's *Svenska Aforismer,* Wahlström and Widstrand, Stockholm, 1951, abounds with wise sayings by famous, and less famous, individuals. He calls his book *ett husapotek* (medicine chest), a place to go to for life's essential needs.

Aside from proverbs, there are sayings about the weather, aimed at informing the farmer of the best time when to perform his tasks about the land. These sayings were gathered in a volume called *Väderbok—Bonde-praktika* (Weather Book—Practical Hints to Farmers), which appeared in Sweden in 1662 in a translation from the German. It contained astronomical data and weather predictions, as well as practical hints for a farm household. According to the book, Christmas weather could be predicted by the atmospheric conditions on the name day of Anders, November 30. Should it thaw on this day, then the day of Tomas, December 21, would be cold and freezing—and vice versa. Snow and rain in late spring were welcome according to the saying, *April snö så gott som fåragö* (April snow as good as sheep manure), and *Maj våt och kall fyller bondens lada all,* meaning that if May is wet and cold the farmer's barn will be completely filled.

Humorous sayings, that have nothing to do with the weather by the way, but refer to the month of April, are the children's jolly quips on the first when they enjoy chanting: *April, april, du dumma sill, jag kan narra dig vart jag vill,* meaning, April April, you silly herring(!), I can fool you into going wherever I want; or *april, april, du dumma fåne, jag kan lura dig ner till Skåne,* which means April, April, you stupid fool, I can lure you down to Skåne.

The chronicles tell that the custom originated from the time when the new year began on April first with the customary exchange of gifts. After the calendar was changed (in 1564), people were apt to forget the new time order and as they expectantly looked for New Year's gifts on the first of April, as had been the custom, they were fooled, naturally, and the sportive mockery was initiated.

# NURSERY RHYMES AND DITTIES

# NURSERY RHYMES AND DITTIES

"Know you then what it is to be a child?" asks the English poet Francis Thompson (1859-1907) in his essay on *Shelley* and gives the poet's answer: "It is to believe in love, to believe in belief. It is to be so little that the elves can reach to whisper in your ear; it is to turn pumpkins into coaches, and mice into horses, lowness into loftiness, and nothing into everything. For each child has its fairy godmother in its own soul; it is to live in a nutshell and to count yourself the king of infinite space."

The play of children is colored by make-believe. And wherever they grow up they skip rope, play hide and seek, and learn nursery rhymes. And they learn to rattle off a succession of words that do not seem to make sense in any language. Nevertheless, these ditties live on from generation to generation. Again, the magic of words. In his imaginary world, a child knows by mere instinct to make an unfamiliar word sound like something he is familiar with. Before he knows what asparagus is, for instance, he may think of it as sparrow-grass, and when rattling off a ditty he has no doubt some association in his head by which he recognizes and remembers it. Perhaps you will recall from your childhood some of these Swedish *ramsor* or ditties which you chanted when counting off playmates one by one in the course of your games:

Essike dessike luntan tuntan
sebuli maka, kukeli kaka
elan belan piff paff puff

\* \* \*

Ettika tettika lonton tonton
simmeli maka kukeli kaka
ärtan pärtan piff paff puff

\* \* \*

The above jibberish can only make sense to those who
use it. In the following ditties an attempt is made to render
a word by word, and line by line translation. To be sure,
some of it defies translation and will serve only as a handle
for recognition and reappraisal of childhood memories.

Äppel, päppel pirum parum.
Kråkan satt på tallekvist,
Hon sa ett—hon sa tu
Ute skall du vara nu
Ja, just du!

Äppel, päppel pirum parum.
The crow sat on pine branch,
She said one—she said two
Out you will be now
Yes, just you!

\* \* \*

Ett två—stå på tå
Tre fyra—kasta lyra
Fem sex—plocka gäss
Sju åtta—liten råtta
Nie tie—slipa lie
Elva tolv—slå näsan i golv

One two—stand on toe
Three four—throw ball
Five six—pluck geese
Seven eight—little mouse
Nine ten—sharpen scythe
Eleven twelve—knock the nose
    against the floor

Tretton fjorton—plocka hjortron

Thirteen fourteen—pick cloud-
    berries

Femton sexton—läs nu texten
Sjutton arton—öka farten

Fifteen sixteen—read the text now
Seventeen eighteen—hasten the
    speed

Nitton tjugu—gå i stuga
Slut—Ut!

Nineteen twenty—go into the cabin
All done—Out!

\* \* \*

Jag ska tala om en saga
Så bred som en tvaga
Och lång som en dörr—
Har du hört den förr?

I shall tell a story
As wide as a scrub brush
And tall as a door—
Have you heard of it before?

Det var en gång en kung
Som kröp upp på en ugn.
Så föll han ner—
Så vart det inget mer!

\* \* \*

Har du ont i magen
Så gå till Per i Hagen
Så lägger han en sten på magen
Så blir du bra i magen.

\* \* \*

Vad ska vi göra?
Ta ett par katter och köra,
Ta svansen till töm
Och köra rakt ned
I Motala ström!

\* \* \*

Tuppen och hönan de voro på renan

Och noppa grönt gräs.
Då kom höken och tog lilla hönan

Och tuppen han grät.

\* \* \*

Skvallerbytta bing bång
Går i alla gårdar
Slickar alla skålar—
Skvallerbytta bing bång.

\* \* \*

Far han var i Kopparberg
Och mor hon satt i stuva.
Far han sålde bort sin märr
Och mor hon sålde luva.

\* \* \*

Ro, ro, barnet
Katten hänger i garnet.
Ro, ro, lilla barn
Katten hänger i mammas garn.

Once upon a time there was a king
Who crawled up on an oven.
Then he fell down—
Nothing more happened!

\* \* \*

If you have a pain in the stomach
Go to Per at Hagen
He puts a stone on the stomach
Then your stomach will be well.

\* \* \*

What shall we do?
Take a couple of cats and drive,
Take the tail as a rein
And drive right down
Into Motala stream!

\* \* \*

Rooster and hen were by the road-
side
Picking green grass.
Then came the hawk and took the
little hen
And the rooster wept.

\* \* \*

Gossip monger bing bång
Goes around in all houses
Licking all bowls—
Gossip monger bing bång.

\* \* \*

Father went to Kopparberg
Mother sat in the house.
Father sold his mare
And mother sold her bonnet.

\* \* \*

Hush, hush, child,
The cat is tangled in the yarn.
Hush, hush, little child,
The cat is tangled in mother's yarn.

Prästens lilla kråka
Skulle ut och åka
Men ingen hade hon som körde.
Än slank det hit,
Än slank det dit,
Än slank det ner i diket.

* * *

Opp och hoppa
Stå ej och dra dig,
När du blir gammal
Vill ingen ha dig.
Sitta i en vrå kan du väl få,
Men mitt unga hjärta
Får du ej ändå.

* * *

Jag skulle sjunga
En liten stump
Om den lilla katten.
Han skulle springa
Efter sin rump
Men han fick inte fatt'en.
Katten sprang och rumpan slang.
Jag skall sjunga den
Än en gång.
Jag skall sjunga
En liten stump
Om den lilla katten.

* * *

Rida, rida ranka
Hästen heter Blanka.
Vart ska vi rida?
Rida sta och fria
Till en liten piga.
Vad ska hon heta?
Jungfru Margareta
Den tjocka och feta.
När vi kom till hennes gård
Så var där ingen hemma,
Bara en gammal gumma
Lärde sin dotter spinna.

The pastor's little crow
Was going out riding
But she had none to drive.
At times it would slink this way,
Sometimes that way,
Sometimes down in the ditch.

* * *

Get up and jump
Don't stand there loitering,
When you get old
No one wants you.
Sitting in a corner you may do,
But my young heart
You won't get anyway.

* * *

I am going to sing
A little tune
About the little cat.
He was going to run
After his tail
But could not get hold of it.
The cat ran and the tail swung.
I shall sing it
One more time.
I shall sing
A little tune
About the little cat.

* * *

Ride, ride on my knee
The horse's name is Blanka.
Where are we riding?
Riding away to woo
A little girl.
What will be her name?
Maiden Margareta
The fat and chubby.
When we came to her house
No one was at home
But an old woman
Who taught her daughter to spin.

"Spinn, spinn, dotter min,
I morgon kommer friarn din."
Dottern spann och tåren rann
Men aldrig kom den friarn fram
Förrn till andra året
Med gullband i håret.

\* \* \*

"Spin, spin, my daughter,
Tomorrow your suitor will come."
The daughter spun and the tear ran
But the suitor never came
Until the year after
With golden ribbons in his hair.

\* \* \*

Bä, bä, vita lamm,
Har du någon ull?
"Ja, ja, kära barn,
Jag har säcken full.
Helgdagsrock åt far
Och söndagskjol åt mor
Och två par strumpor
Åt lille, lille bror."

\* \* \*

Baa, baa, white lamb,
Have you any wool?
"Yes, yes, dear child,
I have the sack full.
Holiday coat for father
And Sunday skirt for mother
And two pair of stockings
For little, little brother."

\* \* \*

The above ditty by Alice Tegnér is representative of children's poetry of later years, as is the following by Astrid Gullstrand:

Visst finns det troll
Små ljusa troll med ögon blå
Och lingult hår
De dansa fram bland oss på tå.
Och ingen vet,
Men ett, tu, tre,
Om vi är sorgsna må vi le
Och taga trollen i vår famn
Och jubla deras kära namn.

För all vår glädje vore noll
Förutan våra små troll.

\* \* \*

Of course there are trolls
Little bright trolls with eyes so blue
And flaxen hair
They dance around us on their toes
And no one knows,
But one, two, three,
If we are sad we have to smile
And take the trolls into our arms
And shout with glee their dear names.

Because all our joy would be nought
Without our dear little trolls.

\* \* \*

A child's prayer that has deep roots and seems to live on in the memory of most Swedish-Americans is the following:

Gud som haver barnen kär,
Se till mig som liten är.
Vart jag mig i världen vänder
Står min lycka i Guds händer.
Lyckan kommer, lyckan går,
Den Gud älskar lyckan får.

God who loves the children
Watch over me who is little.
Wherever I turn in the world
My happiness is in God's hand.
Happiness comes, happiness goes,
He who loves God will have happiness.

Saying grace at the table was often done with these words:

| | |
|---|---|
| I Jesu namn till bords vi gå, | In Jesus' name we go to the table, |
| Välsigna Gud den mat vi få. | May God bless the food we eat. |
| *   *   * | *   *   * |

### RIDDLES

Children like guessing games and riddles continue to excite young minds. Swedish children still knit their brows in an attempt to solve riddles like these:

1. Vem kan tala alla språk?
2. Kan du säga tupp, tupp, och ingen höna?
3. Vad är det som alltid kastas över bord?
4. Runt som ett ägg—räcker runt en kyrkovägg.
5. Vad är det för en väv som kan vävas utan vävstol?
6. Vad är det för en gås som aldrig kunnat kackla?
7. Vad är det som går, men aldrig kommer till dörren?
8. Lilla trille låg på hylla, lilla trille ramla ner.
   Ingen man i Sveriges land lilla trille laga kan.

(Translation and answers in the back of book)

# LUCIA AND CHRISTMAS TRADITIONS

# Julhelg

I årens kretslopp kommer jul
med jämna mellanrum,
och brådska blir i hus och skjul
att feja varje tum.

Är det ett själviskt drag vi ha
att sätta svenskt i topp,
att anse andras jul ej bra
som vår, med vört och dopp?

Visst är det njutbart med kalkon
och allt det goda till,
och ta vi blott ett uns reson
vi slopa ost och sill.

Men dock—vi minnas julens doft!
En egen stämning låg
i skurrent kök, i sal och loft,
en tjusning vi ej såg— '

Och dock så fanns den överallt,
i doft från brygd och bak,
i brådskans steg, i palt och malt,
i allt från golv till tak.

Och se'n när dopparda'n rann opp,,
på takten det drogs in.
En gran blev prydd med flagg i topp—
förtjusta rop: "Försvinn!"

Och julklappskorg blev fylld till rand
och lackdoft stämning göt.
Vår kära far med ivrig hand,
se'n gav oss klapp och nöt.

Förnims en tjusning såsom den,
som höll oss fången då?
Har ljusen nå'nsin tindrat se'n
så klart för stora, små?

Och när vi då väckts upp ur blund,
i ottans gryning grå—
"Var hälsad sköna morgonstund,"
väl aldrig klingat så.

En jul så minnesrik, så glad,
är arv från Sveriges land,
en gåva främst i gåvors rad,
bland svenskar här ett band.

Så låt oss fira jul som förr,
och glädjas åt vårt arv!
Låt julen in i öppen dörr,
ge kärve åt var sparv!

Låt oss ock alltid minnas väl,
att jul gemensam är,
att givandet är julens själ,
om hemma eller här.

**LILLY LORÉNZEN**

# LUCIA AND CHRISTMAS TRADITIONS

In the pre-Christian era the sun was the object of worship and great feasting took place to welcome back its hallowed light. The observance of this pagan festival yielded only slowly to the Christian concept, and Christmas celebration finally became a consolidation of the two ways of thinking. Thus, the festival of the Roman sun god was transformed into a memorial observance of the birth of Christ.

Something of a dedication to the sun is still prevalent among the Nordic people, however. During the long summer days thousands of vacationers do homage to the sun —but for selfish reasons. Not only does it look healthy to have a sun tan, but it is also considered health-promoting to lap up sunshine. And it is felt as a tragedy, almost, if the sun fails to come out during the four weeks vacation which is now due every Swedish employee according to law. This craving for the sun prompts the city dweller to rush out in the country on Sundays and explains in part the scant attendance in Swedish churches during summer months. Parents feel it is their duty toward the children to bring them outdoors and let them have a full day of sun and fresh air.

Inevitably, however, comes fall and gloominess grips the Swedes as the days become shorter. American students studying in Sweden consider November a very difficult

month. Added to the darkness comes the feeling of being
ostracized, they say. "The Swedes isolate themselves—
stay at home with their books and make no effort to
associate." However, comes the day of Lucia, December
13, lights begin to shine and doors are opened. It is the
day that actually initiates the Christmas season and it is
joyously celebrated. Already in the early morning the
traditional Lucia coffee is served. In most Swedish homes
where there is a daughter or young relative, the members
of the household are treated to coffee in bed with the
customary Lucia buns, called *lussekatter*. She is dressed
in a long white robe with a red sash around her waist and
wears a metal crown entwined with green sprigs of lingonberries on her head. The seven lighted candles in the
crown spread a luminous glow around her. It was in
anticipation of such an event that a certain American
student on arrival in Stockholm insisted on securing
lodging with a Swedish family instead of at the student
dormitory. He failed. However, the morning of Saint
Lucia's day became memorable to him just the same. At
his dormitory door appeared new-won friends in hilarious
costumes who served him the traditional Lucia coffee
and buns, and with it much merrymaking.

Here follows a recipe for Lucia buns. They are not
light and fluffy as the American housewife wants her
rolls to be, but rather sturdy in texture. They taste Swedish!

1 cup milk, scalded
1/3 cup butter
2/3 cup sugar
1 yeast cake
1 egg, beaten
3½ cups sifted flour
1 cardamom seed, crushed
Raisins

A pinch of salt

A pinch of saffron, if so desired

Add butter, sugar and salt to the hot milk and stir until dissolved. Cool to lukewarm and add the crumbled yeast cake. Stir well and add the beaten egg. Stir in flour gradually and the cardamom and beat thoroughly. Place dough in greased bowl, cover and let rise in warm place until double in bulk. Knead on a floured board for two minutes. Roll out in small portions and cut into strips about 5 inches long and ½ inch wide. Place two strips in the shape of the letter X and curl in the ends. Place 4 raisins at the center of the bun or one at each curled in end. Place on a greased baking sheet, cover and let rise for 1 hour. Brush with beaten egg and bake in moderately hot oven (400 F.) for 12 minutes, or until evenly brown. Makes 2 to 2½ dozen buns.

From its beginnings as a family celebration, originating in Västergötland and other western parts of Sweden, the Lucia tradition has spread to other regions and is now being observed in most Swedish schools, hospitals, and offices. During the fall a nationwide beauty contest is conducted and the girl chosen is honored in Stockholm as the Lucia queen of the year. Accompanied by escorts, *stjärngossar* (star boys), she arrives at the renowned Town Hall after a triumphal procession through the streets. She is ushered into the Blue Hall, a high-ceilinged main hall, and with great ceremony she is welcomed by city officials and presented with gifts. Eminent distinction is added to the occasion by the attendance of the year's Nobel prize winner in literature who, having been honored on the 10th, usually stays over for the Lucia celebration on December the 13th. It is a distinct triumph for a Lucia queen when she is able to respond in the language of the prize winning author, as he offers his congratulation.

Not only the large crowd present at the Town Hall, but also those that listen in over the radio or watch by television all over Sweden, regard the Lucia celebration as one of the joyful events of the year leading up to Christmas, and they follow Lucia's activities with keen delight. For her it is a crowded day beginning with morning visits to hospitals and orphanages, where her radiant presence makes adults and tots forget pain and sadness, and concluding with the Lucia Ball in her honor. The next day she may well wonder if what she experienced the day before actually was true, or just a lovely dream.

Who was Lucia? The chronicles tell that she lived in Syracuse, Sicily, around the year 300. She had heard of the Christians and became engrossed in their charitable work after her mother had been miraculously healed of a severe illness. Her betrothal to a wealthy nobleman faltered as she became more and more absorbed in giving aid to the needy, even to the point of giving her wedding gifts away. He was adamant in his demand that she should give up her "foolish obsession" and set out to break her resistance. When he failed to exert any influence on her, he turned her over to the Roman prefect who promptly placed her in jail. She was tortured. Her eyes were gouged out with white-hot iron spears, but still she maintained her faith in Christ. When miraculously her eyes were restored to sight, her adversaries were gripped with fear. Finally, she was condemned to death by burning, but even then she escaped and came out of the fire unscathed. Incensed by Lucia's stubborn resistance, her antagonizers, by a crafty device, obtained a magic sword and it was this deadly weapon that accomplished what earlier attempts failed to do. Years later, Lucia was declared a saint and words of her Christian virtues spread to all Christiandom. Her life attracted Dante to praise her as the "One of the Supernal Light," and a celebrated historian, Sigebert Gembloux, wrote an extensive poetic work in glorification of her life.

One may wonder why the western part of Sweden was influenced by the Lucia legend before any other part of the country. The answer may well be that the early missionaries arriving in Sweden came from Ireland. They settled on the nearest western shores and from there continued their preaching to people in near-by places. It was only natural that the life of one of the earliest saints should become part of their teachings. And the legends grew. One version tells that during a famine in Värmland and other parts along the shores a large ship came across Lake Vänern. It was not like any other ship that had ever been seen. At the bow stood a white-robed maiden, encircled by light, and at her command the ship landed along the shore at different points. Large quantities of food were distributed among the starving people. Never had they tasted such fine food. No one but Saint Lucia could bring such gifts. The people who were there claimed that she was, after all, the queen of supernatural beings and she was bound to work miracles.

The word Lucia can be traced to the Latin word *lux,* meaning light. Wherever Lucia is portrayed in art, she carries a lamp or torch, and her head is outlined by a luminous halo. Thus, the symbolism of Lucia is light. According to the Old Style calendar the longest night of the year was December the 13th, which marked the beginning of brighter days to come. Thus, the rugged Vikings feasted and sacrificed to the sun god to hasten the return of the sun. Could it be that through the Dark Ages the first trace of Christianity, glimmering in this new light, was especially acceptable to the Northern people? The answer might be that the Lucia legend coincided with the old pagan belief, which placed light as the most coveted treasure. And to this day light to the Swedes is a life necessity. During the last World War when only a small supply of candles was available in Sweden, it was decided that children and elderly people were to be favored. At Christmas time candles were rationed out accordingly.

By necessity, artificial light plays a great role in Swedish homes during the dark season. Darkness is depressing and through fall and winter it becomes essential to brighten up the inside, so as to counteract the gloom outside. And at Christmas time the profusion of light everywhere makes true the appellation, *ljusets högtid,* or the Festival of Light. Candles are lighted in all rooms and sometimes placed in the windows as a sign of welcome to those approaching the house. An American journalist, who at one time spent Christmas in Sweden, attended *julotta* in a candlelighted church and returned home greatly rewarded, he told a Swedish-American audience later. He had not learned any Swedish, he said, and yet, he had become aware of one Swedish expression that had made a great impression on him. "I heard it so often that I inquired about it," he continued, "and it has to do with candles. The candle itself they call *'ljus,'* but as soon as they put a match to it and it burns they say it is alive and out of this concept they have formed the expression *'levande ljus.'* To them it lends magic to the home milieu. To them it means a warm glow over a festive table and the people around it. To me, too, it meant a mood of festivity and when I entered the candlelighted church on Christmas morning I was gripped by the same spell of holiday spirit. I noticed it in the lusty vigorous singing and in the quiet joy reflected on the faces of the worshippers. By the flickering candlelight I caught glimpses of strong attractive faces and many wrinkled ones, to be sure, and it made me think of a few lines I read somewhere: 'As a white candle in a holy place, so is the beauty of an aged face'."

Looking into a Swedish household a few hundred years ago, we would not have found adequate lighting facilities, and one may wonder how the people accomplished so much in the line of weaving and handicraft as they did. With the open fire as the only source of light, the family members had to crowd around it when doing their spinning, sewing, and carving. Old pictures show how they plucked out a firebrand when wanting to lighten a dark corner. Then came the yard-long resinous wooden sticks called *spingstickor* or *lysestickor,* which had been used in Sweden since the early Middle Ages. At first, they were pushed into the wall between two logs or boards where light was needed. Later they were fastened in iron brackets on the wall. Soon handy fingers carved out blocks of wood and made a slit on top in which the firebrand was inserted. These had the advantage of being movable.

In his *History of the Nordic People* (1555), Olaus Magnus included an illustration of a woman sitting by her spinning wheel holding a lighted stick in her mouth. Beside her is a man with a beer mug in one hand and a basket in the other, also holding a lighted stick in his mouth, and a bunch of prepared sticks in his belt.

When it was discovered that a stick dipped in fat burned much brighter, it was not far to the next step. The stick was exchanged for a piece of twisted moss or tuft of wool—and there was the wick. When the wick was dipped in fat or tallow many times a candle was formed. In 1839 the first factory-made white candles came on the Swedish market.

As early as in 1764, Carl von Linné, the great botanist, writes that firebrands were a thing of the past and used only by *smålännings* and Finns. It is established that

candlesticks were more commonly used at this time. At
first, these were very plain—just a round or square wooden
base with a sharp spike in the center. Tallow lamps were
also used. In time the candlesticks became higher so as
to increase the light radius, and the spike was replaced
with a socket which could be used also for narrower
candles called *ljusdankar*. In wealthier homes candlesticks
of pewter and brass began to appear, as well as those of
china, faience, and silver. In almost every museum in
Sweden such candlesticks are displayed.

Going back to the days when the celebration of Lucia
first began, it was the open fire and firebrands that lighted
up the house during the dark morning hours. Even as
early as three o'clock farm people were up to prepare
the Lucia treat, and there was a stir and hustle to get to
the table quickly. The one who arrived last was called
*lus,* a pun on the word meaning both louse and late-comer.
According to traditions, a war was waged on lice and
vermin around the day of Lucia to make the house clean
and free from defilement for Christmas, and it is most
likely that the epithet *lus* was particularly stinging at this
time.

No doubt, *lussebiten* was more than just a bite of food.
Baking, brewing, and slaughtering were finished and now
was the time for the first taste of the abundant supply of
Christmas food. Sweetened ryebread and saffron buns,
called *lussekatter,* were part of the feast. To this day these
buns are shaped as an X with ends curled out and decorated
with raisins. Speculations as to the name are many. It
has something to do with the traditional belief that evil
spirits were astir, practicing their black magic that night.
It was important, therefore, that all means be taken to
protect and safeguard the household. The devil could take
many shapes—even appear in the guise of a cat—but his

power was nil should the outline of a cat be brought out in the open as was supposed to be the case in the *lussekatter,* or *dövelskatt.*

Not only the people but also the cattle were provided with extra fare. And the ancestral tree in front of the house, called *vårdträdet,* was not forgotten either. On the previous evening some of the newly brewed ale was to be poured over its roots in memory of the generations of kinsfolk who had lived and loved and died on that fa m.

Realizing the firmly held belief of evil powers astir during the Lucia night, one can more readily understand how the radiant appearance of Lucia as the symbol of good was likely to calm anxious thoughts. One of the women members of the household climaxed the feasting by serving the last *lussebit* and with it a hot, spicy drink that later was given the name *glögg.* In time it became customary to serve this hot drink any time during the winter when guests living at a distance arrived after a ride in an open sleigh. Frozen and numb from cold, they were met right at the entryway with a steaming mug of hot *glögg,* which was gulped down on the spot. Today it is a favorite Christmas drink. The ingredients—wine, raisins, cloves, cinnamon, and ginger—are often prepared in a large copper kettle and served in glass cups with blanched almonds.

Lucia, considered the successor to the Nordic goddess Freja, was the harbinger of a good year to come. Had not Freja come to them as an apparition in white during the longest night of the year and served them mead out of a large horn, as the symbol of the good year she was going to bestow on them? The master of the house felt he had sealed the good luck for himself and his household by being generous with food and drink, and he was eager to accept Lucia's good wishes for a prosperous year.

Thus, Saint Lucia came to symbolize benevolence, charity, and good fortune, as well as light.

As time went on the celebration of Saint Lucia's day changed form and ritual. In Trivialskolan, the oldest school on record in Stockholm, observance of the day can be traced back to the year 1655. In *Gamla Stockholm,* one of the earlier works by August Strindberg (1849-1912), dramatist and novelist, written in collaboration with Claes (Klas) John Lundin, a noted newspaper writer and theatre critic, there are quotations from a school regulation regarding the Lucia songs. It appears that it was against the city ordinance at the time to celebrate the day, but at the insistence of the students the school authorities had consented. It is recorded that in 1743 the Lucia celebration began at the school at 6:30 in the morning, when festive candles were lighted in the rector's room, which was gaily decorated with pine boughs. One student from the senior class delivered a versified address in Swedish in contrast to the custom of using Latin. People from all walks of life were present, the story continues, even "the doctor himself," which refers to Dr. Andreas Bergius, the head master.

Today, the Lucia celebration in schools is not restricted. In the university town of Lund, for instance, the students gather at midnight dressed in white nightgowns and march up to the homes of chosen professors. By torchlight they bring their "victims" to *Akademiska föreningen* (a student union) where a Lucia "fest" is being arranged. But first they throw their torches in one heap and leap, one by one, across the lapping flames. It is considered fair to aid a venerable professor in making the jump—for getting across he must!

One reason the students of earlier days persisted in celebrating the day was first of all to mark the closing of the school term, making it a festive *skolavslutning.* Another reason was to impress upon the community that certain privileges were theirs on Saint Lucia's day. It was customary that needy school boys went *lussegången,* that is, they went from house to house singing a gay tune for which they expected, and received, gratuities for their upkeep during the coming school year. This custom was also called *att lussa,* and the practice opened wide the opportunities for others than school boys to disguise themselves and go out "begging." They were called *lussiner* or *lussegubbar* and differed both in purpose and in attitude. They expected to be treated to food and drink rather than to receive a sack of potatoes. Often they were accompanied by a boisterous figure in a black, shaggy fur coat, disguised as *lussebocken* (the billy goat), who with his fearsome buck's head sent shivers of fright into the fainthearted. Fortunately, he was a figure in captivity and his clattering, clanking chains made clear that he was not to be feared, actually. He was Lucifer, the devil himself, who had been conquered by the good Saint Nicholas and was destined to accompany his master on his journey to distribute gifts to the children.

In folk tradition, these symbols of good and evil had a strong appeal, and the impersonation of the generous, loving spirit of Saint Nicholas on one hand and the wicked character representing the devil on the other was perhaps as effective as a sermon. True to nature, Lucifer was not slow in trying his old tricks. Prancing and capering in the procession of merrymakers, he caused shudders of both fright and delight among the onlookers. Before a crowd of adults he played the role of a cunning jester matching wits with them in mutual raillery and banter. Finally, the merrymaking caused so much noise and confusion that it had to be abandoned for a while. After the belief in saints

was relinquished, it was the Christ child instead of Saint
Nicholas who came with gifts to little children and the time
was changed from December 6 to Christmas Eve. But the
shaggy billy goat continued to be a popular figure in the
pre-Christmas celebration and the procession of caroling
merrymakers was not complete without the jesting Lucifer.

How this evil-looking creature in time could transform
into the benign strawgoat of today is one of those peculiar
transitions that only long periods of time can shape.
Perhaps it has to do with the straw that was carried in
to cover the floor before rugs came into use, and the
playful practice of making figures out of it as toys for
children. At any rate, there is a folk tradition from
Uppland that a goat of straw should be brought along
when the merrymakers went out Christmas caroling. This
goat, too, played the role of a jester, often carrying a
"pass" intended for this farm or that, with a humorous
verse on it. Sarcasm could be hidden in the lines referring
to foibles and shortcomings of the recipients, and although
meant as a joke, it had a sting. However, no one was
supposed to take offense. Often a straw doll accompanied
by an amorous verse, thrown into the home of a young
girl, served to convey the feelings of a bashful suitor. The
shaggy buck called Lucifer had become harmless and the
making of straw goats and other articles of straw is a
flourishing business in Sweden today. No one ever regards
the Christmas goat as anything but a decoration or play-
thing.

The time between Saint Lucia's day and Christmas
Eve has always been marked by hustling feet and busy
fingers. Not only should all the baking and food preparation be done, but the house should also be cleaned from
attic to cellar. Poor father would feel rather homeless at
times, although he had his duties too. The Christmas

tree should be brought home and the snow plowed and shoveled. And for all, there were the Christmas presents to finish. When time was getting short, mother would announce *en oppsittarkväll,* which meant that all the members of the family, and sometimes invited friends, would sit up late one evening working on their presents. It was a common concept that a present was worth far more when it was sewed or knitted or carved by the giver himself, and numerous were the writing table mats, pillow tops, *brickband* (strips for holding trays), mittens, stockings, scarves, and breadboards in the making during those pre-Christmas days! In order to keep secrets secret separate rooms were used throughout the evening, until the coffee, chocolate tray, or the fruit bowl brought the busy workers together.

School boys often knitted mittens or garters for their female relatives. In order to get money for material great sacrifices were made. Christmas gift money did not come easy. This brings to mind how the boys in our family each morning sacrificed the two pieces of sugar they were entitled to for their cup of chocolate and saved them in a jar. Towards Christmas they sold the sugar back to mother, who paid well. What they did not know was that mother, taking one look at the thumb-smudged sugar lumps, quietly dumped the sugar in the garbage pail. The lesson of sacrifice was learned, however, and a giddy ecstasy was part of it.

What is the interpretation of the word *julklapp?* Several explanations are offered. It may have originated from the early custom of delivering Christmas presents anonymously with only a clap or *klapp* on the door and then hastily departing. The idea was not to be seen. He was considered smart who could push the present in through the half opened door with one sweeping gesture and then escape

without being discovered. Most of the time this was not
possible. Hospitality ruled that no one must leave the
house without a treat, so hustling feet were at once in
hot pursuit, and in most cases the visitor was brought
back to have a taste of the Christmas fare. Some scholars
object, however, to this interpretation, maintaining that
rural people never used the word *klappa* in this sense, but
said *bulta* or *banka* instead, whereas *klappa* was common
in the expression *klappa henne på kinden,* for instance,
meaning a soft pat or caress on the cheek. Whatever the
origin, the custom of giving presents was a common one.
Often the gifts were insignificant as value goes, or they
were gifts of a humorous nature.

To the needy, one would give a goodly share of the
accumulated Christmas food. Came Christmas Eve, the
cattle did not go without an extra ration either. And the
last sheaf of grain saved at harvest time for the birds was
placed high on a pole outside the windows, or up on the
roof. It was said that these feathered visitors would eat
less out in the barn if they had their own sheaf to plunder.
Another tradition maintains that it looked prosperous to
be openhanded with the grain in this manner. But there
is a deeper significance, say the initiated. In the sheaf was
the essence of the harvest, the vital power that makes
grain grow, the spirit of fertility itself. There was magic
around the last sheaf gathered up after the threshing was
done, or the last sheaf brought in from the field. Sometimes the stalks had been pulled up by the root and then
carefully tied together into a tight, solid sheaf. All the
generating force and energy lay hidden in it, according
to the old belief. Saved until Christmas, it was given to
the cattle on Christmas morning as a special treat, or
else placed outside the house to emit blessings to all who
lived there and to all who came visiting. The birds took

advantage, incidentally. Sometimes it was placed in an apple tree to induce *skördeanden* (the spirit of harvest) to bring a good crop. In western Sweden the name given to the sheaf brought in last was *löktnek,* which comes from the verb *lykta,* meaning to finish. It was carefully braided, leaving a bushy top-knot, and used as a decoration in the house. At Christmas time it was placed outside for the birds to plunder, or given to the cattle for extra energy.

If the last sheaf contained a magic power, how much more powerful was the meal milled from its grain. A special bread was baked of it called *såkaka* or *såddkaka,* which first decorated the Christmas table during the holidays and then was put away and not touched until spring. It was then hard and dry and had to be pounded or ground into crumbs before part of it was portioned out to man and beast alike as a magic fare, which was supposed to provide strength and vigor and a sense of general well-being. The remainder was mixed with the seed-corn and planted with visions of burgeoning crops later on.

The baking of Christmas bread was an undertaking of great proportions because of the need of large quantities. Aside from the baskets of bread for the poor, and the supply to be put away for the winter months, each member of the family was to have his or her stack of breads called *julhög.* This was to contain a sample of each kind of bread baked at Christmas, and it could be nibbled at and tasted at will. The custom hints of the time when food was scarce and regarded as *ett gudslån,* meaning a loan or gift of God. But at Christmas time all efforts were made that each individual would have enough food to eat. And bread was the essence of life, was it not? Much of this concept is still prevalent in Sweden, and many of us remember from childhood the stern parental order always to eat a piece of bread with each morsel of other food

items. And if you happened to drop a piece of bread on
the floor you had to pick it up at once—and eat it. Beware
that you should ever step on it! What happened to the
girl in Hans Christian Andersen's fairy tale when she
stepped on the bread? Remember?

The Christmas bread was often baked in the shape
of animals. In Småland it was customary to bake a bird-
shaped bread and further north it was shaped like an ox.
According to skill, goats and pigs were also shaped out of
the dough. A common name for those bread figures was
*julkuse.* One may wonder what prompted this custom.
Some scholars maintain that it reflects the old belief in
sacrifice when during pagan times animals were slaughtered
to appease the gods. In the case of poor people who had
no animals to offer, animal-shaped bread was substituted.
Whatever, Christmas was a belated harvest festival and
it was only natural that bread came to play a great role in
the celebration.

Whether it is the special Christmas bread called *vört-
bröd* (made with malt extract), or *limpa* which is round
and sweetened with molasses and orange peels, or any
other kind of bread that calls forth nostalgic cravings, we
all must agree that nothing will ever be as delightful in
the same way as the aroma from the kitchen when mother
hurried with her baking, or the first bite out of a freshly
baked loaf of bread at Christmas. Not to mention the
seven kinds of cookies. That was a fragrance of another
kind. No self-respecting Swedish housewife would have
less than seven kinds of cookies in her house, and often
more. *Pepparkakor* (ginger cookies) were baked first
because they would keep the longest, and then followed
*mandelmusslor* (a fluted almond cooky, by Norwegian
tradition called *sandbakelse*), *strutar* (brittle cornucopias
which during the holidays were served filled with jam

and whipped cream), and all the rest that defy translation. Delight and fascination would shine from the eyes of so many children and they would watch how the cookies were stacked in jars and placed on the highest shelf of the pantry. A hesitant *"Snälla mamma, får jag en kaka?"* (Mother, please, may I have a cooky?) would yield only broken pieces or those cookies that happened to be burned.

To the Swedes, Christmas, more than any other holiday, is the time for sentiment and joy. Stored feelings come out in the open and the freedom to express what is in the heart is joyously embraced. No one need fear being considered emotional or sentimental, because everybody is prompted by the same feeling. This release of emotions makes for a warmer companionship, and at no other time of year, perhaps, are there such gratifying attachments formed as at Christmas. The formality is put on the shelf and the Christmas spirit takes over.

To the children the anticipation is almost unbearable. They count the days—the day before the day, before the day . . . —until at last the day itself arrives, Christmas Eve. That is the day of climax in Sweden, not Christmas Day. Weeks of scrubbing, weeks of baking, weeks of cooking terminate with this day. The house smells Christmas! The kitchen is trimmed with frilled paper streamers in red and white. The Christmas tree is brought inside and with it fresh air and a scent of pine. The children flock around father as he puts the star at the top of the tree and mother searches through the boxes for the familiar trimmings. Flags from foreign countries as well as the blue and yellow flag of Sweden are fastened, and it becomes a jolly game to try to remember which country is represented by the different flags. And the frilly candy decorations! A vision of fringed tissuepaper in bright colors comes to mind and clumsy fingers trying to fasten narrow gold strips around the so called *papperskaramell*. It was the children's task to make these decorations, but that which should go inside the paper—caramels, gumdrops, or other sweets—often landed in the mouths of the "decorators." Last of all the small candles were fitted into the wire holders and an apple placed on the hook below to give weight and balance. And each year it was the most beautiful Christmas tree that anyone had ever seen.

In the kitchen busy hands had been stirring since early morning. *Dopp i gryta* is in the making. The expression means dip in the pot, and involves a ceremony. But first to the ingredients. In the large kettle a ham bubbles and boils, and as the hours advance the sausages are added, such as potato sausage, cream sausage, pork sausage, and sometimes a piece of rolled meat, called *rullsylta*. The broth, smooth and shiny with fat, gains in strength and substance. When the ham is cooked through, it is removed and rubbed with brown sugar and mustard and studded with cloves. After a brief glazing in the oven, the ham is ready and the meal can be announced. The time is generally twelve or one o'clock and the table is set in the kitchen, even though the house may have ample room for dining elsewhere. *Dopp i gryta* must for all practical reasons be eaten in the kitchen. Serving the meal buffet style facilitates the procedure, or ceremony, in front of the stove where members of the household now gather to dip their bread in the pot or *gryta*, that is, in the hot broth. This custom goes back to pagan days, it is told, when the vikings at the time of the winter solstice, and dreary with the darkness, sacrificed to the sun by fasting, that is, refraining from eating meat and making a meal of bread and broth only. One can assume that the thick broth yielded enough strength for husky bodies to endure until the sun god was appeased and began his journey back.

For modern consumption the meal, with meat, is satisfactory indeed, and washed down with dark, foamy Christmas ale leaves nothing to be desired—for a while. At the coffee table later on, all the seven kinds of cookies are brought forth, tasted, and commented upon, while the children hang around wondering if *jultomten* (Santa Claus) will ever come. Eventually he does arrive, dragging his sack with him, filled with Christmas presents. *"Finns det några snälla barn här?* (Are there any nice children here?) he asks. Are there ever any but nice children at Christmas?

So begins the distribution of gifts and within minutes the room is a sea of billowing tissue paper and bulky wrappings. If the family is one of adults, it is customary to prepare humorous rhymes for each package, and the reading of these verses furnishes added enjoyment to the moment of giving. Jokingly it is said of many a Swedish writer that his talent was discovered by his rhymes on Christmas gifts. Elaborate wrapping paper has caught up with Sweden but people who keep to old traditions use brown paper and red sealing wax. The procedure of heating the wax over a candle flame, letting it drip down on the knots of string, and then stamping one's own seal on it to make an imprint, was a fascinating ritual. And the mood and atmosphere of Christmas, by Swedes called *julstämning,* is surely at hand when someone in the house begins sealing his or her Christmas presents. The fragrance of the melting wax makes everyone aware that the awaited moment soon will come.

The final meal on Christmas Eve is by tradition *lutfisk* and *risgrynsgröt* (rice porridge), preceded by a light *smörgåsbord*. *Lutfisk* can now be bought under this name, at least in Minnesota, and is prepared and ready for the kettle. In Sweden, only a generation ago, the housewife

had to go through the procedure of preparing it. On the
day of Anna, December 9, the dry fish was placed in a
lye bath and then rinsed and turned regularly until Christmas Eve when it was considered to be just right. Unless
one knew exactly how long the fish should boil, there was
danger of overcooking, in which case the quivering *lutfisk*
would put on a vanishing act and leave only bones and
skin behind. To those Americans who are introduced to
Swedish customs by marriage, the eating of *lutfisk* is said
to be the most trying. The very smell of it is enough, they
say. Many a resolute mother-in-law has hit upon the idea
of boiling the fish ahead of time or in a closed off base-
ment room, and has succeeded in convincing her newly
won son or daughter that with a generous amount of cream
sauce, melted butter, salt, and pepper it is not bad at all!
If fish it must be . . . *Gröt* is easier to take, however, and
if the one single almond, which a pot of rice must contain,
happens to land in the plate of the in-law, the evening is
made. He or she will be rich and prosperous during the
coming year, says the myth. Should the almond turn up
in the plate of a single person, it means marriage within
the year.

At last the most important day of Christmas comes to
a close and a weary but happy housewife sighs and anticipates the morrow when nothing but rest is in store for
her. There is no big turkey dinner to prepare and seldom
any company to fuss for. Christmas Day is the first day
after several weeks of intense work that she can relax, and
she depends on her family to bring the ham and the
sausages and the bread on the table, knowing that there is
food enough for the keenest of appetites. But first she must
summon her waning strength for an early rise for *julotta*
(Christmas service). . . . Where is the alarm clock?

Attending *julotta* in Sweden is to many Swedish-

Americans one of the most treasured of memories. Snow is connected with it and sleigh bells and a journey across the countryside in the dark morning hour, brightened by the flickering flames of torches. Many have memories of a city church within walking distance, and they remember with no less feeling of nostalgia how the snow crunched under the feet and how the light streamed out of the windows as they approached the church. Thus, each one of us gathers memories out of the milieu from which we come. But to all of us the message of Christmas and the singing of "Var hälsad, sköna morgonstund" (literally, be greeted beautiful morning hour) constitute common ground. This hymn is still numbered 55 in the revised hymnal of the Swedish State Church, and the manner in which it is sung each Christmas morning indicates clearly that the congregation knows it by heart. A Minnesota professor of Swedish descent, now deceased, maintained that it was a mistake to sing this hymn in an English translation. It had only one version, according to him, and that was the Swedish. "That is the way I learned it as a child and that is the way I continue to sing it regardless of what the rest of the congregation sings," he would say with an emphatic nod.

Each one who has attended early Christmas Day service in a Swedish church could write his own version and each one would be different from the other. A University of Minnesota student who studied in Stockholm a few years ago was a guest of relatives in Skåne at Christmas and attended *julotta* in a small church there. He gave his impressions of the holidays in a letter this way: "My relatives were among the most generous, most warm-hearted, kindest people I have ever known. They seemed so happy to have me and I enjoyed myself so much that I stayed a whole week. There was plenty of food in Skåne!

One day I counted seven times at the table. Christmas
Eve dinner was eaten by candle light. I insisted on going
to *julotta,* and as they had no car I walked the three miles
to the nearest church, the kind of church I had always
dreamed of worshipping in for *julotta* in Sweden. It was
set on a high hill in a small village and with the lights
from candles, the village Christmas tree lights, and the
candlelight from all the village houses, the scene was visible
for miles around. It was quite fantastic—a Danish-type
church, whitewashed, red tile roof, stepped front, and
eight centuries old. The inside, lighted with candles, was
decorated with evergreens and two large Christmas trees.
*'Var hälsad, sköna morgonstund'* could never have had a
more beautiful earthly setting. The minister himself was
quite marvelous—well padded with good Skåne food, so
that his heavy jowls made his bib pop up and down as
he preached. His sermon on Saint John's chapter on The
Light was meaningful and presented in a personal, ordinary
tone not always characteristic of Swedish pastors. As I
walked home through the Minnesota-like woods and hills,
the sun came up and I realized that it had been a long
time since I had felt such peace and satisfaction."

*Levande ljus* also makes the memory of the dead alive
at Christmas. It is customary in many parts of Sweden to
light candles on the graves of those who have passed away,
and since rural cemeteries often are located around the
churches, it is done in connection with the services. Flickering flames in the snow on a dark morning is an impressive
sight.

According to tradition, the dead attended *julotta* ahead
of the living, and many people as they arrived in church
fumbled stealthily with their fingers over the bench before
sitting down in order to discover the speck of dust and
gravel they expected to find there. One can not get out

of a grave without leaving some marks behind, they meant. Looking sanely at the situation, people began to realize that children who crawl up with their feet on the seats could very well have left earth and gravel there, and that old churches often deteriorate and shed sand and small particles of building material, especially with sharp temperature changes. Still, the old belief was slow in yielding. Selma Lagerlöf makes vivid this old conviction in her story *Mamsell Fredrika—En julhistoria,* which tells of Fredrika Bremer's midnight Christmas service, of her attendance at *julotta* twice that year in 1865, and of her death a week later, mourned by all Sweden and by many throughout the world.

While Christmas Day is strictly for the family, the next day, called *Annandag jul,* is for visits and parties. In the old calendar the day commemorated the first Christian martyr, Stefanus, and in the Swedish almanac of today it is marked Stefan, sometimes spelled Staffan. Since all farm work was at a standstill on Christmas Day, it was necessary to be up early the next day to clean the barn and tend to the cattle. It was customary that the young sons and farmhands extended their services to favorite neighbors, who in turn would treat them to food and drink. Originating with this custom was *staffansritten.* The horses had to be taken out for watering and their tenders would give them a brisk workout by riding them to the neighboring farms. Soon they were joined by riders from other places and the ride developed into a lively race. As they came thundering up into the farm yards, doors were thrown open and treats offered.

The farm chronicles tell of the customary Christmas feasts beginning on *Annandag jul* and the special arrangements of a gathering place for young people. It was customary that the farmer who granted facilities to the young people also in part furnished the food, whereas the drinks and whatever else the meal was to include would be gathered up during the day by "Staffan's stable boys," the young farmhands who simply went begging from farm to farm. Others who served as collectors of food to the party were the so called star boys, dressed in their dunce-like hats, and others disguised as spooks. One begins to understand the necessity of preparing barrels of food for Christmas when one considers the great number of solicitors and "beggars" waiting at the door for handouts. But open hand and open heart was the symbol of Christmas, and joy and laughter was in the air as young people as well as old gathered to eat and dance and play games.

*Ringdans* was always a part of the evening's fun and as the participants joined hands forming a circle, they sang the words to the old dance tunes with zest and gusto. Inside the circle one or two couples performed the action in the song. The accompanying fiddlers would mark time by tapping a foot and the dancers would emphasize the beat with brisk steps as they kept the circle moving, while all the time the romantic interest grew and boy and girl got better acquainted.

The custom of Christmas parties continues. We who were brought up in Sweden remember those occasions with fondness, although it may be that we tend to overrate such events. At any rate, there were many of them during a holiday season, all evaluated according to youth's emotional bent. Some were fun and others were dull, we thought. However, on entering the host's house there was a fragrance from the lighted candles on the Christmas tree and from candles everywhere else, and one felt immediately in tune with the spirit of hospitality. Guests in their Sunday best warmed their hands before the flaming fire in *kakelugnar* (porcelain stoves) or open fire places, and the air seemed charged with dizzy anticipation. As all were friends and neighbors, the conversation soon became a lively buzzing, and as more and more guests arrived the spirits of the company rose.

Youngsters were usually assigned to one room and there the Christmas games took place. But first there were sidelong glances at the festive table where bowls of fruit were set out, and big platters with nuts of all kinds and dates and chocolates in fancy wrappings. The utmost in taste sensation was *teaterkonfekt,* we thought. It was made of almond paste and shaped into apples, pears, and berries. With the true coloring such pieces looked very real. Furnished in fancy, crinkly paper bags, they were sold from aisle to aisle during intermissions at a theater performance and that is how the name originated. Now a taste of such delicacies was in store for us.

No one went near the table, however, until the hostess called out, *"Var så goda allesammans!"* And not even then were the youngsters allowed to make a move towards it. There was a long wait while the grown-ups filled their plates and the host busied himself with serving the hot spicy drink called *glögg.* How could it take them such a long time! Finally, it was the youngsters' turn and with hungry glances they took in all the unspeakable delights of the table. With a little coaxing, however — had not mother warned that they must not grab at the first urging of the hostess—they would help themselves, bow or curtsey, and retreat to the seclusion of the room assigned to them. Well inside the door, all timidity would vanish. While chattering and laughing they ate and munched, some sitting on the floor, others wedging in on the chairs. The clatter of nutcracking accompanied the chatter and suddenly a shrill voice would call out *"filipin!"* It meant that a double almond had been found in an almond shell and when a

partner volunteered to play *filipin* with the finder of the
almonds, it was decided how high the stakes should be.
Often it was merely a question of a treat at the pastry
shop (*kondis*) or a piece of chocolate. The one who called
out *filipin* first when the two met again, a day or a week
or a month later, won the game and got the treat. Many a
romance began with such a "game."

As the evening progressed, some of the men would
gather in groups engaged in conversation, others would
stand before the fire talking, while the ladies sat together
exchanging views on favorite recipes and the cares of a
household. And to be sure, the one ranking highest on the
social ladder would sit in the center of the sofa, holding
court, so to speak. It is amusing to recall how mother
sternly admonished her daughters never, never to sit on
the sofa when at a party!

Soon one could sniff a delectable aroma coming from
the kitchen, revealing that a late supper was in the making.
To youngsters the anticipation of good food was exciting,
as well as the prospect of staying up late and with it the
feeling of being grown-up—almost! For some reason an
invitation to a Christmas party did not always make clear
whether it would be a late supper party or just an evening
gathering, and youngsters would make it a guessing game
to determine what was in store. If not supper, tea and
openfaced sandwiches were served later in the evening.
In that case, no delicious whiffs would drift in from the
kitchen—and spirits drooped. It would be a "dull" party.
But, in anticipation of a supper, playing became livelier
during the evening and the game of forfeits offered many
incidents conducive to romance.

Finally came the magic words, *"Var så goda!"* The
table was a display of tempting dishes. But as before, the
youngsters had to wait until the grown-ups had supplied

themselves with a taste of this and a taste of that. Aside from the usual array of herring and small, boiled potatoes, there would always be an omelette filled with creamed mushrooms or asparagus, meatballs, fish loaf with lobster sauce, and a number of platters with cold meat. The host would toast his guests and extend a greeting of welcome to all, if he for some reason had not done it earlier. The informed Swede knew that the *smörgåsbord* was only the beginning, and after a while the main course would be brought in—either roast pork loin with stewed prunes or a veal roast, perhaps. Boiled potatoes, a ubiquitous item on a Swedish table, and creamed vegetables would accompany the meat. A dark, foaming ale would be served with the meal.

Finally, after hours of eating, it seemed, the dessert came on the table. Often is was a large torte, or red berry pudding called *kräm,* or preserved ginger pears with whipped cream. On rare occasions the meal would end with ice cream. To this writer nothing could equal ginger pears, however. At one Christmas party when I did not have mother's watchful eyes over me, as she was home sick in bed, I ambled out in the kitchen where busy women ran about preparing the food. When I wanted to know what the dessert was going to be and was told it would be *kräm,* I simply announced: "When my mother has a party she always treats to ginger pears and whipped cream." At the time I did not understand why I was grabbed so roughly by the shoulder and set down quite unceremoniously in the next room. The incident was promptly reported to my mother and the reprimand was severe. But I still favor ginger pears and cream!

After supper someone would sit down at the piano, the tree was pulled out from its corner, and all joined hands. To the old tune of *"Ja, nu är det jul igen"* (Yes, now it is Christmas again) the dance around the tree went on and on to a lively beat. Sometimes it would ebb out in a snake dance through the house, upstairs and downstairs, until the breathing for some of the older people became labored and the singing collapsed with a burst of loud shouts and happy laughter.

All agreed it had been a jolly party and soon the guests would crowd around the host and hostess to say goodnight and express their thanks. After having found the wraps in the outer hall, family by family would step out in the crisp starlit night, well pleased and eager to breathe in the fresh air. And father would mutter something about how nice it was to get a little walk after all the eating.

Memories are individual and based on personal experiences. But it is commonly agreed that there was genuine *julstämning* over our childhood's Christmas holidays. To many it stands out because for once there was enough food to go around. To others there was the sensation of smelling the scent of Christmas, of being gripped with the joy of giving, and seeing the transition of the house from everyday wear to festive holiday dress. Perhaps it was a pair of new skates or a lovely doll that made a particular Christmas so memorable. Perhaps it was simply because we were so young. . . .

**A NEW YEAR**

# A NEW YEAR

As the new year approaches, the Swedish people glance through the new calendar, called *almanack,* for information on various matters. Published annually, it furnishes the latest reports on social insurance, military service, post and telegraph fees, passports, time of sunrise and sunset (Stockholm), the subject for each Sunday's church service, and much more. Should one want to know how old the queen of Sweden is and how many names she has, it is there, as well as the same information on all the members of the royal family. And speaking of names, the common man has his name there, too, that is, if he was given a common Swedish name at the time of his baptism. Each day of the year lists a name—with a few exceptions—and the namedays of those persons within one's circle of relatives and friends must be remembered as if the day were a birthday. Earlier it happened, but nowadays more seldom, that a new-born child was given the name of the day of his birth. As a youngster grew up, he would soon realize that he had been deprived of a nameday—and protested. As a child this writer could not quite forgive her parents for giving her a name that was not even listed in the *almanack.*

Feminine names of agelong tradition appearing in succession in the *almanack* are Sara, Margareta, Johanna, Magdalena, Emma, and Kristina. These names, beginning on the 19th day of July, make up the week called *frun-*

*timmersveckan* (the woman week) when, according to
old weather signs, the rain falls continually. Even if it
sometimes came true, the celebration of these namedays is
not in any way hampered and the coffee parties follow
one another all through the week.

One of the days without a name is *Allhelgonadagen,*
November first, meaning All Saints Day, and another is
*Menlösa barns dag* (Innocents' Day), December 28,
which commemorates the Herodian massacre of Bethlehem
babes.

Epiphany or Twelfth Night, in Swedish called *Tretton-
dedag Jul,* is celebrated on January 6 as a legal holiday. Old
chronicles tell of the pageants performed at this time, por-
traying the three Wise Men, Mary and Joseph, and the
Christ child accompanied by the star boys, called *stjärngossar,* and a mysterious figure with a large pouch called
*Judas med pungen.* From their beginnings as church
dramas these performances changed into processional pre-
sentations, having merrymaking and revelry as the main
purpose.

Not until the day of Knut, January 13, or *tjugondag
Knut* (twenty days after Christmas), do the Swedish people
feel that the holidays are over. The expression *att dansa
julen ut* refers to the custom to dance Christmas out of the
house, so to speak, or dance around the tree for the last
time. It is said that in earlier times it was customary for
friends and neighbors to gather in each other's homes and
finish what was left of food and drink. Nowadays it is the
children's day celebrated with a party called *julgransplund-
ring,* when the youngsters "plunder" the tree of all its
goodies. If the eatables should have "disappeared" during
the holidays, mother will place a new supply of sugar
plums, marzipan pigs, and chocolate soldiers on the tree,
so that the plundering can be performed with actual gain.

After the tree is completely "robbed," the children watch a bit soberly as it is dragged out and thrown into the yard. Not until this moment is Christmas definitely over. The whimsical little rhyme that says it will last until Easter states in the next line that it is not true, because in between comes Lent.

Preceding Lent, the Swedish calendar designates two other holidays. On the first Sunday in February the Swedish church observes *Kyndelsmässodagen* (Candlemas Day) or the festival of light, which has its origin in the time of Catholic rule in Sweden when the priest distributed candles to his parishioners for the purpose of safeguarding them from the power of the devil. The service, called *kyndelsmässa,* was named after the Latin word *candela* meaning light. Today candles still play a role in the services. The young people attending confirmation classes usually gather at vesper time and walk in procession through the church carrying lighted candles.

The day is also called *Jungfru Marie Kyrkogångsdag* in commemoration of the first visit to the church by the Virgin Mary after the birth of Christ. The old Jewish law stipulated that forty days should elapse before a mother could visit the temple after the birth of a child, the idea being that before that time she was unclean, or unworthy. The custom, accepted by the Christian church and in Swedish called *kyrktagning,* is not observed today.

Until 1952, the day of the Annunciation of the Virgin Mary, in Swedish called *Marie Bebådelsedag,* was a legal holiday celebrated on March 25. By a parliamentary ruling it was moved to the Sunday nearest the date. In compensation for the lost holiday, another day was designated as a legal holiday, namely the first Saturday in November, called *Allhelgonadagen* (All Saints Day).

Since Annunciation Day comes about the time of the

vernal equinox and signifies the transition from winter to spring, it has traditional significance. *Tranan bär ljus i säng* is an old saying, indicating that from now on one can go to bed while it is still daylight. And it is *tranan* or the crane, now returning from a warmer climate, who gives the promise of spring to come. In southern Sweden this bird is held dear, and the day of its return is greatly anticipated by the children. A recent contributor of personal experiences from childhood days in Sweden writes: "For a long time I imagined that the crane came flying with a large candelabra in its beak and lighted candles in its claws. After we children had gone to bed—by daylight —we tried to lie awake so that we could watch when the crane would come flying in through the open window. But Jon Blund (the sandman) caught up with us. However, we knew in the morning that the bird had been there, because he had left gifts by our beds, often figs, oranges, and dates which vividly proved to us that he had been in that mysterious, tropical country where he was supposed to go each fall."

Another custom at this time of year was to run barefoot, bravely defying the discomfort of a wet, cold ground. The purpose was to develop strong feet, to protect oneself from snake bites and other injuries, to reap a good harvest, and so forth. And the route was set—either around the house three times or to the nearest farm and over the farmer's heap of manure, across so many fields, etc. Friends and neighbors made bets and saw to it that the running was carried out in good order.

Annunciation Day is also called *Vårfrudagen* (the day of Our Lady), in the vernacular transposed to *vafferdagen*. This in turn has been interpreted *våffeldagen*, indicating that waffles are the traditional fare of the day. In order to conform to all customs, the waffles should be baked in a heart-shaped waffle iron in remembrance of the Virgin Mary's heart, but a standard iron will do as well! In some parts of Sweden it is also customary to eat *vaffergädda*, meaning pike. It is easy to catch the fish as the lakes throw off their cover of ice. The saying is that *gäddan öppnar gapet,* that is, the pike opens its mouth.

Aside from special food, Annunciation Day brings a keen anticipation of spring, of longer days, and warmer weather. And who is going to be the lucky one to find the first *blåsippa?* The little blue anemone is the symbol of spring itself. Its competitor, but more common, is *Tussilago farfara* or coltsfoot, in Swedish *hästhovsört,* which seems to shoot out of the ground with its yellow crown on the very first warm day in spring. The children compete with each other in the effort of being first in bringing spring flowers to their favorite grown-ups. And they know the names of the flowers, because it is generally obligatory for children to learn both the Latin and the Swedish names of plants, at least in the secondary schools.

Another sign of spring is the return of *sädesärlan,* a black and white bird that runs about wagging its tail, in English called just wag-tail, and the swallow. And there is a thrill in hearing the first warblings of the lark. But on hearing the measured call of a cuckoo bird for the first time in spring, a Swede would stop in his path, stand erect, and listen.

Often when listening to the first cuckoo call, a Swede would determine from what direction it came. If he is superstitious it counts! *Norregök är sorgegök, östergök är tröstegök, södergök är dödergök, men västergök är bästergök.* Thus, from the west the call must come to bring the best tiding. From the north and south only sorrow and death lie in wait for the listener, but from the east comes comfort and consolation. According to folk humor the whimsical bird may answer life-determining questions, such as how many more years one will live, how many children one would have, or how many more years one has to go unmarried. Should the unreasonable bird answer with a number of calls, one could interpret it as a jolly joke, but if he would fly away without any call at all, the questioner would have reason to pause.

The cuckoo bird has peculiar habits. He is a polygamist, he builds no nest, and slips his eggs into the nests of other birds, who have to hatch them and care for his offspring. Therefore, to say about an unreliable, untrustworthy person that he is *en riktig gök* is a tell-tale verdict. Still, the cuckoo bird is the harbinger of spring and much is overlooked. Even outings are arranged around his arrival. Members of a club or society, or simply a group of young nature lovers would gather early in the morning with baskets of food and coffee jugs—in case it is not feasible to make an open fire and cook the coffee on the spot— and settle down in a lovely glen or meadow and there quietly await the first morning call of the cuckoo. The suspense is great, the listening intense. Not until the rhythmic call has echoed through the woods is there any thought of preparing breakfast. But when the silence is broken, happy voices ring out and the "table" is set with a nice cloth on the grass. Everybody enjoys the early breakfast in the open, and after many cups of coffee, someone may begin humming a familiar tune and before long everybody is singing. Perhaps someone will bring an accordion to accompany the songs, and also furnish music for ring-dancing. The early sunrise, the fragrance of flowers and new leaves, and the companionship of a group of convivial friends make the outing a memorable occasion. And the time is short. As soon as the cuckoo bird sees the first haycock, he stops calling and the wait is on until next spring to hear him again.

As nature dresses in a new crisp spring attire, so does the Swedish home. Housewives invade each room with scrub brushes and soap and male members of the household scamper about feeling lost. But as clean curtains begin to appear in the windows, they sigh with relief and move back to their favorite chair. By then all the *innanfönster* (inside windows) are removed—in Sweden the storm-windows are put inside—plus that wad of cotton with trimmings of *eterneller* (strawflowers) that during the winter has given an illusion of warmth and perhaps kept some draft out. Elis in the play *Påsk* (Easter) by August Strindberg gives expression to his delight over such a situation as he arrives home on a slushy spring day: "Innan-fönstren ur, golvet skurat, rena gardiner, ja, det är vår!" (The inside windows are out, the floor scrubbed, clean curtains, yes, it is spring!

**EASTER CUSTOMS**

# EASTER CUSTOMS

"When is Easter this year?" As the new year begins we are curious about the date, and although we know that Easter Sunday cannot come earlier than March 22 and not later than April 25, and that it falls on the first Sunday after the first full moon following the vernal equinox, we do not feel certain until having looked it up on the calendar.

Lent, commemorating Christ's forty days of fasting in the desert, was early established by the Christian church as a time when the faithful refrained from eating meat. It was not easy to convince the Northern people of the necessity of this observance, and the chronicles tell of the grumbling and clanking of sword on shield as their king urged compliance with the law. Farmers complained that fasting weakened them and therefore prevented them from working in the field, and even the monks found that the meager fare kept them from carrying out their sacred duties. Surreptitiously, it says, meat was included in their diet.

However, during the Catholic times in Sweden there was before Lent a time of furious unbending and feasting called *fastlagen*. This term is possibly a distortion of the German *Faselabend*, which at first signified just the evening before Lent began, but later included several days. Thus, one distinguishes between *fastlagen*, which is the time before Lent begins, and *fastan,* signifying the time of fasting before Easter.

The roguish pranks and mischievous merrymaking which identified the carnival as celebrated on the European continent found expression also in Sweden, as is evidenced by a recorded statement from 1527 in which King Gustaf Vasa expresses concern that he would be subjected to ridiculous foolery, *såsom mångom androm skedt är* (as has happened to so many others). Court jesters in disguise would by pranks and frolic play tricks on high and low, and sometimes make themselves odious by their affronts. Practical jokes were also common among the country people. In Skåne, for instance, they would place a cat in a barrel and make a game out of it. Participants would be horsemen, dressed in a white linen shirt, blue homespun pants, a gay-colored band around the waist, and a paper helmet on the head. Each man also wielded a wooden sword or an old hussar's sabre. The barrel holding the cat was hung up, swinging freely between two poles, and then the onslaught of the riders began. One by one they attacked the barrel, trying to break it with one stroke of the sword as they were riding by. The one who succeeded in freeing the cat was pronounced cat king. Carl von Linne' wrote about this custom: *Då får han taga vilken han vill av pigoskaran till drottning; härpå dansas med andra menlösa nöjen,* which means that he could choose any girl he wanted as his queen and thereafter there was dancing and other innocent diversions.

In northern Sweden young people gathered before Lent with their sleds and *sparkstöttingar* (chair toboggans pushed along like a scooter) covered with as many sleigh bells as they could find. The idea was to make as much noise as possible, and as the crowd congregated on a high hill everybody shouted and jingled the bells. As the long train of sleds rushed down the hill, there was the added burst of excited voices and gay laughter. The ride was called *att åka stora rovor och långt lin,* alluding to the superstition that great crops of turnips and a good harvest of flax would in time be forthcoming. Needless to say, the outdoor merrymaking was followed by profuse feasting, and sometimes a dance.

Every Tuesday during Lent it is customary in Sweden to eat *fettisdagsbullar,* also called *fastlagsbullar* or *semlor,* which is a round bun with a smooth unsugared top. It is scooped out and filled with marzipan and placed in a soup plate. Hot milk is poured over and the dish is eaten as dessert. Is that good, one may ask. To some people it is, and to the rest of us it is no treat whatever. Modern medical science declares it is even harmful. A warning finger is pointed to the case of King Adolf Fredrik, who suddenly died (in 1771) after having eaten the bun. Scrutinizing the case, however, one finds that preceding the bun the meal included sauerkraut, smoked meat, lobster, caviar, and smoked fish, all washed down with champagne. Topping off the meal with *hetvägg* (at that time the name for the roll) and hot milk, proved his undoing, says the chronicle. A contemporary courtier remarked, "Det är ej att omkomma på det mest lysande sätt," meaning: One could die in a more glorious manner, to be sure.

How *fettisdag* or fat Tuesday got its name goes far back in time. With the restriction of food during Lent, people became hard to handle and the grumbling disturbed the authorities. So, in order to ease the regulated abstention, a fat piece of pork or two were allotted on Tuesdays. This extra ration perked up the spirit and fasting for another week was made more palatable.

The first day of Lent, Ash Wednesday, was dedicated

to penitence and repentance. As a visible sign the faithful
would smear ashes on their foreheads, which remained
until the Thursday before Easter, called Maundy Thursday,
when the ash marks were washed away and the soul was
considered cleansed as well. Aside from being a day of
purification, Maundy Thursday was also a time of communion and the master of the house saw to it that all
members of his household went to church.

Much superstition was also connected with this day.
Witches were astir and it was necessary to keep all doors
closed. And it was important not to lend anything or give
anything away. For further protection all thresholds and
door posts should be smeared with tar and the sign of the
cross be marked out everywhere, even on the noses of the
cattle. It was believed that witches needed animals to ride
on for their journey to Blåkulla, the fictitious mountain
where the devil awaited them for a secret conclave. In
addition, these witches needed glowing amber from the
fireplaces and butter or ointment in their horn—better
close the damper quickly. . . . Had not the people of old
seen them ride on their broomsticks through the sky with
the black cat, the horn, the *kaffepetter* (coffee pot), and
with their hair flowing in the wind? And had not grandmother told in her days about the elaborate feast the
witches had each year with the devil himself, and about
the wild dancing afterwards to the music of croaking
magpies? Oh, those birds—everybody knew they were
away over Maundy Thursday!

So ignorance and fright conjured forth an image, until
witches became real and the whispering began. A menacing
finger would first point out one and then another of the
women in the neighborhood. One could never be sure
who was the guilty one because a witch could disguise
herself and escape recognition, although she lived on the

next farm. On Easter Sunday, for instance, after their return from Blåkulla, the witches would attend church service as other parishioners. There was one way, however, by which one could distinguish them. With forethought, one could put three chicken eggs in the pocket or else a four leaf clover in the stocking, and upon arrival in church all would be revealed. And lo and behold, there sat one and there sat another, so easily distinguished by the wooden milk pails on their heads!

The imagination of churchgoers who could neither read nor write was stimulated by the pictorial scenes painted on walls and ceiling, and as long as the spoken Latin words failed to catch their interest, the religious motifs served to occupy their minds. In Yttergarn church in Uppland there is a painting from 1480 showing three Easter witches ready to take off for their journey to Blåkulla. A magnificently depicted devil fills their horns with the magic drink from his own large vessel. This picture is said to be the oldest version of Blåkulla-destined travelers in existence in Sweden. An extensive study of the art of mural paintings in Swedish churches has been done by Henrik Cornell and Sigurd Wallin, resulting in valuable publications. The three latest volumes deal with paintings in twelve churches in Uppland, two in Dalarna, and one each in Medelpad and Västmanland.

It seems incongruous to us today that this superstition should have led to the cruel trials recorded as having taken place in Dalarna, Hälsingland, and Bohuslän in the seventeenth century, when many innocent women were by torture forced to a "confession" and then put to death. As late as 1720 a woman from Värmland was accused by a twelve-year-old girl of being a witch. And remarkable it was. . . . The girl told that she had been compelled to accompany the woman to Blåkulla! An investigation

was made and "Captain Elin" and ten other women were
imprisoned at Örebro castle. The governor intervened,
however, proving that the confessions were elicited by
starvation and torture. Captain Elin's witchcraft symbols
are now in safekeeping at the Nordiska Museet in Stockholm, including such things as a horn, a foot of a rooster,
a bear claw, and a broomstick to which three leather
tongues are attached.

In modern Sweden the witch motif has endured and
finds a humorous expression in Easter cards and table
decorations, not to mention live performances by children.
They love to dress up as Easter witches (*påskkäringar*).
They daub their little faces with red, put on a long skirt
and a bright kerchief on their heads, and fortified with
a long broomstick and a horn, if they can find one, or an
old copper coffee pot, they start out in the neighborhood
and run from door to door shouting, *Glad påsk* (Happy
Easter)! They linger long enough, however, to receive the
expected treat. This custom is observed especially in
western Sweden and in the suburbs of Stockholm. Another
custom which is observed by youngsters of school age is to
deliver Easter messages. These are vividly colored drawings, done by the children themselves, depicting a witch
crawling out of a chimney ready to take off, or in full
flight on her broomstick through the air, with a fanciful
black cat and all the paraphernalia needed for a meeting
with the devil. Anyone clever with a rhyme would enclose
a little pertinent stanza. Folded as a letter, these drawings
are delivered at dusk on the Eve of Easter at the door of
schoolmates, and it is important that one does it without
being discovered.

Another Easter motif is the feather-trimmed birch
twigs, which serve as a table decoration during the holidays.
They are sold in "bouquets" at market places with the

tip of each twig tied with tufts of feathers in different colors. The riot of colors displayed at Hötorget in Stockholm, for instance, all through Lent, is eyecatching indeed.

Stripped of their modern feather trim, the birch twigs become the dreaded *påskris* (Easter switch) of old, used on Good Friday to give the children and servants of the household a few beatings to remind them in a tangible way of the sufferings of Christ on the cross. In Strindberg's play *Påsk* the birch twig is prominent as the symbol of chastening. In almost every household there was *riset,* a tight bunch of birch twigs placed behind the tile oven or in a corner somewhere, ready to be snatched out when the occasion called for a reprimand. *Vill du smaka riset?* (Do you want to have a taste of the switch?) were dreaded words, and sometimes only a glance at it was enough to make children behave. Because it did sting!

Good Friday, in Swedish called *Långfredag,* is still a solemn holiday in Sweden and in childhood memories the longest day of the year, just as the name indicates. All grown-ups were dressed in black, making them look very somber, and we children had orders to sit quietly with our books hour by hour. We were forbidden to touch steel, such as a needle or a pair of scissors—it would violate the memory of Christ's suffering on this day. We were not allowed to go out. No one came calling. In the morning mother had given us a playful little slap with the birch twigs to remind us of what day it was. As if we could forget! This somber mood was so instilled in the Swedish mind that many an immigrant Swede was shocked when he learned that in America stores and shops were open on Good Friday and that the day was regarded as a workday.

To illustrate that the Good Friday mood and attitude are still prevalent in some circles in Sweden of today, this little incident may be told.

A few years ago, a Minnesota student studying in Stockholm went down to Skåne for his Easter holidays and decided to call on a fellow student he had met earlier in the year, who had urged him to come visiting whenever in the vicinity of his home. As the American tells it, he was greeted with coolness and formality, so different from the gay mood which had marked their meetings previously, and he was greatly puzzled at the change in his friend's behavior. That Good Friday had anything to do with it never occurred to him. As the family thawed out and the guest began to feel more at ease, he was told that Swedes do not expect callers on Good Friday and that was the reason why he had been met with constraint. As he tells it, he enjoyed his visit and was treated to a lavish meal— but never again on a Good Friday, he vows.

On Easter Eve in southern Sweden, just at dusk, the big bonfires begin to blaze. In every village young people have been busy gathering tree trunks and branches and dried up bushes and shrubs into a great heap. If a barrel of tar can be added, so much the better, and the sound of the crackling fire would mingle with loud bursts of voices cheering each flame as it rose above the others. Now and then a bit of gunpowder would explode with frequent crackling bangs, and shots into the air would add to the noisy merriment. Singing and dancing around the fire would be another part of the game, and sometimes the watch would last until daybreak. The idea in olden days behind this noisy custom was to chase the witches away. The clergy thundered and preached against superstition, at the same time making vivid the evils of the devil. It is told that in 1715 a few young farmers from Västergötland had been guilty of firing shots at Easter, but after having declared explicitly that no superstition was involved, they were set free. Another farmer in another parish was not so lucky. His penalty was one sheep from his flock to be given to the poor.

Why are eggs such a predominant fare at Easter? A natural explanation would be that after forty days of fasting, when no eggs were to be included in the meals, it was a special treat to indulge in egg-eating without restrictions. Another reason may be that the supply of eggs is more plentiful in the spring. At any rate, the standard fare to this day is boiled eggs and the idea is to eat as many as can possibly be consumed. In some homes this feast is scheduled for the evening meal on Easter Eve, but in our home it was at breakfast on Easter morning. It was too much for the digestion to eat many eggs at night, mother said. Finally the morning came. How exciting it was to see the large kettle on the stove and father taking out his watch to mark the time, and to see how dozens upon dozens of eggs were immersed into the boiling water. With seven children around the table quantities of bread and butter and milk were needed, too. Although we were allowed to eat egg after egg, as many as could go down, the rule held as always—"eat bread with your food, children!" So with each egg bread and butter had to go along, and even so one Easter my oldest brother ate sixteen eggs! That he was ill the rest of the day was miserable, of course, but he had come out the winner.

Often it was the custom to write humorous rhymes on the eggs, and these were read at the table. They were, to be sure, naive and simple, but served to bring out the cheers: *Ut ur ägget vill jag hoppa, och på grönskan börja noppa* (Out of the egg I want to jump and begin to pick at the green) or *Detta ägget det ska smaka, hoppas att jag inte spiller på min haka* (This egg will taste good, hope I don't spill on my chin). It would be interesting to collect such rhymes used through the years when a big family gathered around the table at Easter.

In medieval times it was customary to bring eggs and
other food items to church in order to have the priest bless
them. When the old altar cabinet was torn down in Vamb-
lingbo church on Gotland in 1901, the Latin text of a
prayer was found, entreating the Lord to bless his creation,
the eggs. Today youngsters in Skåne roll eggs down the
sandy dunes along the coast and shout with glee when the
eggs collide and spill all over the slope. The high sea wall
north of Kivik in Skåne is still called *Äggabackarna* or the
egg hills.

Another custom with eggs is *äggapickning* observed in
Simrishamn. The fisher folk and harbor habitues gather
on Easter morning with hardboiled eggs in their pockets,
eager to start the game. Two players stand opposite each
other, one holding his egg still and the other using his
for attack. The rule is strict—end to end, never the sides.
The winner is the one whose egg is unbroken after the
assault. There is a lively banter in the crowd and *äggapickning* continues far into the day. For those who lose their
eggs there is always a youngster with a basket of eggs,
ready to replenish the losses.

To a Swede, much of the enjoyment of Easter is his
anticipation of spring. He thinks of his boat and how it
needs to be scraped and repainted, and of the first balmy
day when the family congregates with tools and paint and
a coffee basket to help father get their beloved boat ship-
shape for those eagerly awaited jaunts on the lake or
along the coast.

**WALPURGIS NIGHT**

## WALPURGIS NIGHT

On the last day of April, called *Valborgsmässoafton* in Swedish, spring is officially greeted in song by white-capped university students, who celebrate the event with solemnity —which later on gives way to a spirit of abandon. In Uppsala the tradition prescribes that the winter head-gear is thrown into the Fyris river, and precisely at three o'clock in the afternoon, the assembled crowd of students don their white velvet caps and cheer the arrival of spring. And cheer they do and sing throughout the next twenty-four hours while the caps remain on their heads. In the evening, they march with banners and flags waving up to the slope below the castle where the chosen speaker delivers the speech to spring. The traditional student chorus sings while the twilight lingers, and under the sea of white caps thoughts grow sentimental. Much has been written on the romantic mood of such an evening. Seldom do the words catch what the moment holds, however.

At the student club houses, called *nationer,* the students gather for supper and dancing until sunrise, when it is customary to eat a herring breakfast. By then it is the first day of May and the rest of the townspeople are awakened by the sound of blaring band music. To the tune of *"Sköna maj, välkommen"* (Beautiful May, Welcome), early risers march in procession through the streets. This occurs in other Swedish cities, too, but in the university towns of

Uppsala, Lund, Stockholm, and Göteborg, students carry out the academic traditions. The new university in Umeå is quickly adopting the pattern, and from place to place echoes the traditional student song, *"Sjung om studentens lyckliga dag,"* followed by the four resounding cheers to spring.

A Swedish student, visiting in Minneapolis one spring, failed to find any one sensitive enough to the importance of celebrating *Valborgsmässoafton* in a proper manner, and in desperation she aimlessly went on a shopping tour in a large department store. Above the row of elevator doors there is a clock and as the time approached three she stopped in front of it. As she told it, there were mixed thoughts sweeping through her mind as she stood there being buffeted by the milling crowd. How could they know what a giddy feeling it is to celebrate spring in Sweden! Now she was in the United States—but traditions had to be carried out. She pressed the paper bag close to her side and watched the minutes go by. Now, precisely three o'clock and out flew the white student cap from the paper bag, and with four loud ringing cheers she coquettishly placed it on her blond head. Oh, yes, people stared she said, but at that moment she was gripped with such joy of being young and having spring to anticipate that she did not care.

The name Valborg, which occurs on the first day of May in the Swedish calendar, commemorates a saint of that name who died in Germany around 776. On the day of Valborg in earlier times it was customary to say a mass in her honor, and *Valborgsmässoafton,* which falls on the day before, signifies the eve of the mass or *mässa.* The old superstition of witches being astir on this night may have originated the tradition of building huge bonfires, because the fluttering flames were supposed to chase them away.

There was also a belief that the fire would scare away wild animals. These were much feared in view of the fact that on May first the cattle were brought out to pasture. Today, no belief in witches prompts the Swedish people to gather in the sometimes chilly evening around the fire. It is a practical way of getting rid of trash and rubbish, and whatever can be found of brushwood and sticks of all kinds are added in the attempt to make the fire flash and crackle, and emit sparks that can be seen far and wide. Young, strong voices join in singing the traditional spring songs. Often there is dancing, while an individual merrymaker may run around firing a shot or two. In some parts of Sweden it is customary to put on a spectacular display of fireworks.

*Att sjunga maj i by* (to sing May into town) is an old custom from southern Sweden. On the last day of April young men would gather with a few musical instruments and large baskets and walk from farm to farm singing their May song. As a reward, they received eggs in their baskets for the *ungdomsgille* or feast they were arranging later. Another custom was the nationwide call to arms for inspection and display of marksmanship, which took place on the first day of May. This military tradition originated in Rome in the ninth century, was adopted by the townspeople on the European continent, and finally came to Sweden where it developed into an annual rally, when not only marksmen congregated but also great crowds of spectators. It turned out to be a *folkfest*. Today, the first day of May is a legal holiday in Sweden, and great gatherings are still the custom. It is a day of political demonstration when long processions of different units of citizens, carrying their flags and banners, march through the cities to a designated place where an invited speaker gives an address. To be true, it is no longer a demonstration or an expression of revolt as it was in earlier years. For after more than thirty years of social-democratic government, the ideals of workers' rights and social justice have been successfully realized, and the May Day parade has become a peaceful expression for a prosperous people marching ahead. Not that the text on the banners does not call out for shorter workdays, more subsidies, etc., but it is not done ostentatiously. Many an older, conservative Swede, as he stands there watching the procession go by, would mumble something about the welfare state being pretty prosperous the way it is compared to what it was in his young days. Time marches on, though. . .

**MIDSUMMER FESTIVITIES**

## MIDSUMMER FESTIVITIES

*Midsommar!* To a Swede the word holds joy and visions of sunny meadows, shimmering waters, the rhythmic beats of an accordion or a fiddle, dancing around the maypole, and a sun that at midnight seems to linger by the horizon, only to rise in full blaze again. Perish the thought of rain at midsummer! And in this inviting milieu festive holiday crowds respond wholeheartedly to nature's own festival. The summer solstice brings daylight all night long, decidedly so in northern Sweden. Every family, every individual anticipates the occasion eagerly and one common urge grips all—to be outside, whether by a lake shore or in the country. All work is abandoned; picnic baskets are packed. Relatives and friends congregate; young people get acquainted. Is it any wonder that one of the early emigrants from Sweden working his first year as a hired man in the United States expressed his disgust, almost unbelief, when he learned that he had to work during midsummer. *"De va ett uschlit land—håller de inte ens helgera i ära?!"* (What a wretched country—don't they even respect the holidays?)

To the many who cannot flock to the country, the cities offer varied opportunities for a midsummer celebration. A flower-bedecked maypole is raised in a park or open place and often there is dancing in the streets, even without a pole. Stockholm, the summer city par excellence, has

Skansen, the large wooded park located on a hill over-
looking the city. As related earlier, here one can spend the
whole day and evening dancing, listening to concert music,
walking through the wooded area and looking into the old
cottages from different parts of Sweden, watching the
animals in the zoo, or just sitting at the summit of the hill
and marveling at the view below. And when hungry, one
has a choice between a good meal cafeteria style, a more
formal dinner at the main restaurant, or simply a cup
of coffee in the open air cafe. Skansen is Stockholmers'
*sommarnöje* (summer pleasure), unique in its varied means
for relaxation and enjoyment.

But it is in the country that the midsummer celebration
with its agelong traditions comes to its liveliest fulfillment.
And it is mostly around the maypole that the festivities
take place. The word *majstång* (Maypole) has nothing
to do with the month of May, although the custom *att maja*
involves spring foliage. It means to decorate with green
leaves and branches, and at midsummer this is done with
abandon. Not only is the Maypole trimmed with garlands
of flowers, but every house and dwelling gets a row of twigs
around the front door. Sometimes young birch trees are
placed on each side of the entrance. Boats are trimmed with
leaves, too, and motor cars as well. Inside the house the
open fireplace is filled with fresh green foliage and vases
are supplied with wild flowers from the meadow.

Under a shady tree the long coffee table is set, the cloth
bedecked with flowers. To partake of food any place but
outside is unthinkable. As friends and neighbors gather,
the festive mood is running high and soon busy hands are
tieing garlands around the Maypole. Flower garlands are
made and fastened with colorful ribbons to the crossbar.
Often a rooster is placed at the top of the pole, or a crown-
shaped flower trim, or a long banner. In coastal regions

of Sweden the pole is often trimmed with small sailboats, hanging down from the crossbar. In other areas the trim may be flower wheels of different sizes hanging by ropes from the top.

As strong arms heave and push, the Maypole is raised on a grassy open place and all the celebrants, young and old, join hands and dance around it to the gay tunes of an accordion or a fiddle or two. As more people gather, double circles are formed moving in opposite directions and, according to the tunes played, nimble feet keep changing steps and move briskly in time with the music. And everybody sings! The words to the old tunes are known by all, and the singing accompanies the performance of the couples inside the circles. The song or ballad often portrays the rivalry between a lover and a rejected suitor, and it is up to the performing couples to make the drama vivid and convincing. As the tune ends, other couples step into the circle and repeat the melodrama. To dance in this connection does not imply only dancing as we think of it, but *ringdans,* actually a movement of song and play. It is naturally a favorite pastime during the summer when young people get together in the country or in a city park.

While the daylight lingers, the midsummer festivities continue throughout the night. After the ring-dancing, the crowd may stroll over to an open dance floor built up among the birch trees, or to a farmer's barn, festooned with birch twigs. And for those living along the shores of Sweden—sturdy docks lend themselves very well to dancing. After a summer in Sweden, an American student boasted: "I have danced on every dock in Bohuslän!"

For a fleeting moment around midnight as the sun dips below the horizon there comes a hushed silence. Nature seems to hold its breath — even the birds stop

twittering. The earth and all growing things drink in the
dew and send forth a heady scent. It is *skymning* or twilight. Boy and girl strolling hand in hand are part of the
picture as the midsummer night casts its spell. It tricks
even the sedate and solid participants into a brighter mood
and older people claim that such a night is a sure cure for
old age!

At last it comes to an end. As lovers stroll arm in arm
towards home, the sun is high in the sky. An unattached
girl takes the way through the meadow where she picks
a bouquet of seven kinds of flowers. At home she places
them under her pillow, hoping to dream of the man she
one day will marry.

Hugo Alfven (1872-1960), the beloved Swedish composer, captured the mood of a midsummer eve in his
composition *"Midsommarvaka,"* which depicts in music
the lively dancing of the early evening, the hush at midnight, and the resumed dance rhythm as the sun bursts
forth over the horizon. Part of this music has been adopted
in this country under the name "Swedish Rhapsody."

In the wintertime, twilight comes early in the afternoon
and denotes a prolonged transition between daylight and
complete darkness. It often marks the time of day when
busy fingers smooth out the apron and hands come to rest,
and the whole household takes a brief recess. At least,
those are my recollections of childhood. *Att kura skymning*
meant to sit quietly and watch how the outlines of familiar
objects in the room grew dimmer, while mother told a story
or an episode out of her own life. As the darkness deepened
we felt safe and warm and comfortable to have mother so
near—and idle. But all of a sudden she would announce:
"It won't do to sit like this!" And as she lighted the lamp
mood suddenly changed. It was time to begin studying the
lesson for the next day.

So, summer or winter, the time of twilight entices. The only part of Sweden where twilight is at a minimum is in the North at midsummer when the sun remains in the sky for over a month.

The timing for the celebration of midsummer has been changed in recent years. Earlier the date for the midsummer day was June 24, marked in the calendar as *Johannes Döparens dag* or the day of John the Baptist. Now the day is celebrated in connection with the weekend closest to the original date. To a sunstarved people this holiday, next to Christmas, is the most eagerly anticipated and planned for, and when it comes, most joyfully celebrated.

# WHEN IN SWEDEN VISITING . . .

Do not neglect to shake hands! Do it when saying hello and when saying goodbye. If you are a house guest shake hands with your hosts in the morning when you come down for breakfast, and again at the end of the day when saying good night. Add the ingratiating words: *Tack för i dag!* (Thanks for today.) Thus, you thank your hosts each day you are under their roof and in addition after each meal when it is appropriate to say *Tack för maten!* Shaking hands is a must also when meeting anyone. And it is customary for a woman to offer her hand as readily as does a man. When arriving at a party, one shakes hands with everyone present, and says his name at the same time since the host might not have the chance to introduce all the guests. A name is mumbled in response, but often one is still in the dark as to who the person is because of the inarticulate way the name is said.

Do not leave food on your plate, if you can help it. Food is seldom portioned out on individual plates but served from platters, so you may decide yourself how much you can eat. If the wine is already served when you sit down at the table, do not touch the glass until the host extends his words of welcome in a *skål.* Even if you do not approve of wine, it would be a gracious gesture on your part to bring the glass to your lips as the toast is proposed. This ritual is part of social life in Sweden, observed also by teetotalers, who use fruit juice as their table drink instead of wine. You may make your wishes known beforehand that you would prefer a non-alcoholic wine. As the dinner progresses, more toasts are proposed. At the end of the meal, the male guest of honor seated to the left of the hostess will give a toast of thanks in behalf of himself and other guests for the dinner. Sometimes such speeches are eloquent and humorous, lending gaiety and animation to the party. Coffee will be served after the meal in the living room.

Do not put on your wrap until you have said goodbye to the hosts. This will seem only natural as your coat was placed in the entrance hall or *tambur* as you came in, and there you will find it on your way out. You will not be invited to place your coat in a bedroom.

Do not neglect to sew a strap or loop at the back of the collar of your coat, by which it can be hung up on a hook. In homes you will find hangers, but not in public places. Going to a concert or the theatre, you will leave your wrap in the cloakroom where the attendant, after having fumbled for the loop and not finding any, will be forced to drape your coat over the hook. It facilitates service to comply with the loop.

Do not overlook the importance of saying *tack för senast* to your hostess a day or two following a party. By this you thank her for the entertainment at her house. The courtesy of telephoning your hostess and thanking her for a "lovely party" is one of the social graces that will assure you of an invitation again. If telephoning is not convenient, a written message will do as well.

Do not enter a restaurant of distinction expecting to be served speedily! To spend an evening "out" is an event to a Swede and he settles down to enjoy it to the hilt. You will notice that most public dining places in Sweden have an atmosphere of quiet, subdued animation where time runs into hours, and the pleasant conversation in the company of good friends is enhanced by the milieu itself and the distinctive food served with elaborate care.

Do not enter a "Bar" with the idea of having an alcoholic drink. These places are snack bars where milk, coffee, tea, and quick meals are served.

Do not turn your back when entering a crowded row in a theatre or movie house en route to your seat. Face the occupants you pass by and murmur a discreet *förlåt* (sorry).

Do not crowd in when trying to get on a bus. The custom is to stand in line and await one's turn.

Do not stay on the curb side when escorting a woman companion, unless it coincides with the rule that a gentleman stays on the left side. Walk to the left when meeting pedestrians. Sit to the left of a woman in a vehicle.

Do not hesitate to use the telephone for long distance calls for fear of the expense. Sweden is the telephoning-est country in the world with thirty-two telephones for every hundred inhabitants. You can do much telephoning for less than a dollar! And the operator speaks English. An initial call costs two ten-öre coins.

Do not—and this above all—do not drive a car after having consumed alcoholic beverages. The penalty is stiff.

Do not neglect to register with the local police department on arrival. If you stay at a hotel this matter is taken care of by the hotel office. When staying with relatives or friends who live in the country, notify *Landsfiskalskontoret* of that district. If you intend to stay longer than the three months your passport allows, you must apply for a residence permit, called *uppehållstillstånd*. This can be done through *Statens Utlänningskommission*, Birger Jarls Torg 5, Stockholm C., and will cost four kronor for one month's stay, six kronor for one to three months, and twelve kronor for a period exceeding three months. The telephone number is 23 31 20. In staying in larger cities where there is an American Embassy or Consulate, it is wise to register your name and address there also, facilitating mail and other messages. American Express is another point of contact which may prove useful.

In conclusion, it may be said that many a friendship between a Swede and a foreign visitor has come about through the initiative of the latter. So why not be bold and introduce yourself, if the occasion arises. Often the Swede would like to take the first step but is too timid and staid to do so. More often than not he is happy to meet you and happy that you have broken the ice. This is especially true if one is an American because Swedes expect Americans to be more outgoing. Do not become discouraged if some Swedes fail to respond. In cases where they do respond it will be more than rewarding. As has so often been said—to have a Swede for a friend means a lifetime of friendship.

# TRAFFIC FROM LEFT TO RIGHT

The present right-hand traffic in Sweden was changed from left-hand driving in 1967. Loud voices had long been clamoring for the transition, but the opposition maintained that the cost would be prohibitive. On May 10, 1963, the Swedish Parliament made the decision for the change.

The only countries in Europe adhering to the rule of left-hand driving were England and Sweden. With the rest of Europe driving on the right and the increase in tourist travel to and from Sweden, it became more convenient, to be sure, and a great deal safer when Swedish traffic conformed to that of the rest of the continent. The exceedingly fine highway called Europa Route 4 has opened a direct motor lane to the continent, which channels traffic throughout Sweden from Haparanda in the north to Hälsingborg in the south and continues as far as Lisbon, Portugal. As automobile traffic is increasing with each year and thousands of tourists from other countries motor into Sweden, especially during the summer months, it becomes more and more evident that the new ruling is the only way out in promoting a smoother flow of traffic.

The speed limit within towns and other communities is as a rule 50 kilometers an hour, or 31 miles.

The highways leading in and out of towns and cities are paved and well marked. Smaller roads in the country often have a smooth gravel surface. The cobble-stoned,

narrow streets in older cities are not conducive to modern
motor traffic. In the oldest part of Stockholm, called
Gamla Stan, the streets are so narrow that an approaching
vehicle will send pedestrians scurrying to the side streets,
or force them to stand flat against the house wall while
it passes. On the business street called Västerlånggatan all
motor traffic is prohibited, giving the shoppers a chance
to walk freely in the street and view the display windows
on either side.

Parking areas inside the city limits are marked by
a sign with a large P on a yellow background. If this letter
appears with a slant through it, do not park!

The Stockholm streetcar and bus system is modern and
efficient. And although the city suffers from congestion
during the rush hours, one may get from one part of town
to another in a relatively short time by public transportation. All sections of the city are afforded convenient
and frequent service.

If your destination is near a subway station, use this
new and popular way of transportation. A sign with a
large blue T (*tunnelbana*) on a white background can be
seen from quite a distance and indicates where to descend.
To locate the right train is easy, as long as you know in
what direction you are heading. To go west, for example,
simply follow the sign *tåg västerut.*

The stations are called along the way and plainly
marked. They are brilliantly lighted and in some places
handsomely decorated in multicolored tile. Other stations
abound with posters advertising varied kinds of mer-
chandise. An array of small shops, each beautifully dis-
playing current commodities, makes the concourse and
entrance hall of the main subway stations colorful and
interesting.

# TRANSLATION OF PROVERBS

from page 183

1. Just right is best
2. Pride goeth before a fall
3. A burnt child shuns the fire
4. The world's reward is ingratitude
5. New brooms sweep best
6. Opportunity makes the thief
7. One gains wisdom through suffering
8. A hearth of one's own is golden (worth gold)
9. Little pitchers have big ears
10. Being away is fine, but being at home is best
11. He who does evil fares evil
12. One swallow does not mean it is summer
13. As you make your bed, so you must lie on it
14. When in Rome do as the Romans do
15. Do not cast pearls before swine
16. What is hidden in snow comes forth in the thaw
17. Strike while the iron is hot
18. When the cat is away, the mice will play
19. Small children, small worries—big children, big worries
20. When gruel comes raining down, the poor one has no spoon.

# TRANSLATION AND ANSWERS TO RIDDLES

from page 194

1. Who can speak all languages? The echo.
2. Can you say rooster, rooster, and no hen? Rooster, rooster.
3. What is it that is always thrown over board (board also meaning table) The tablecloth.
4. Round as an egg—reaches around a church wall. A ball of yarn.
5. What kind of weaving can be woven without a loom? The spider web.
6. What kind of goose is it that never was able to cackle? Butter goose, which is a literal translation for sandwich.
7. What is it that runs but never gets to the door? The clock.
8. Little roly was lying on the shelf, little roly rolled down. No one in the land of Sweden can fix little roly. The egg.

# ACKNOWLEDGEMENTS

This book is the fulfillment of an ambitious undertaking and a labor of love. The idea of writing it has come and gone during the years until in the spring of 1961, at the completion of sixteen years of teaching Swedish at the University of Minnesota, it became persistent and begged for action. Giving voice and impetus to this idea was Dr. Theodore A. Olson, professor of Public Health biology in the College of Medical Sciences, University of Minnesota, who attended my spring class at the American Swedish Institute in anticipation of a leave of absence to be spent in the Scandinavian Countries. Stimulated by hearing again of the Swedish traditions and customs as presented in this class, Professor Olson urged the instructor to make them available in written form. The task seemed enormous. But strongly encouraged, I left for Sweden later that spring to collect material for my project. I am deeply indebted to Professor Olson and sincerely hope that the result of my work will justify his confidence in me. For his initial prodding and continued interest I express my most sincere thanks.

While in Sweden, it was my privilege to have the counsel and advice of Dr. Albin Widen, who during World War II managed a Swedish Information Bureau in Minneapolis. As a dedicated scholar and writer on *Svensk-Amerika*, he took special interest in my project and read my manuscript chapter after chapter as it came out of the typewriter. I am very grateful to Dr. Widen for his valuable help and suggestions.

Mrs. Carola Goldkuhl, John Ericsson scholar and author, and Miss Karin Lundgren, teacher in Stockholm's public schools, were also kind enough to read the first draft of the manuscript. I express my sincere thanks to them for their helpful observations.

To Professor Hans Zetterberg of Columbia University, New York, I extend my deep appreciation for his interest in my project and for reading my manuscript. His observations have also been very helpful and his comments encouraging.

I owe much to Mr. Peter S. Jennison, executive director of the National Book Committee, New York, and author, for his devoted help in my search for a publisher. His professional advice served me well indeed and I express to Mr. Jennison my most sincere thanks and appreciation.

I want to extend my special thanks to Mr. Allan Kastrup, for many years director of The American-Swedish News Exchange, now the Swedish Information Service, in New York, for his expert help and counsel during the writing of this book. I value greatly his interest and support.

Sharing my responsibility for presenting to the publisher a manuscript as free from errors as is humanly possible is Mr. Clifford Jensen, a graduate of the University of Minnesota and a former student of mine. After a year's study at Stockholm University, Mr. Jensen returned with a fluent command of Swedish. He is the student mentioned in connection with the Lucia festivities and the Christmas celebration in Skåne, as well as the speaker appearing at Skansen when a proverb saved the day. Mr. Jensen is now a publications editor for Honeywell Inc. As he says himself, he has not changed the contents or the style of writing, so if the phrasing at times seems quaint it is entirely my own acquired way of using English. And I would rather have it that way than to present a more polished text that would not be mine. I am deeply indebted to Mr. Jensen for his invaluable help in editing the manuscript as well as his assistance in proofreading, and I express to him my warm and most sincere thanks. Without his professional help the book would have suffered greatly.

From the embryonic stage of a book, when it is only a small glowing pinpoint of an idea, to the final concrete reality of cover, print, and pages the road is long and sometimes dreary, sometimes breathtakingly smooth and fun to travel. In retrospect, it does not seem long to me, although three years have passed. Often I have been beset with doubts. Where could I find an American publisher who would have foresight and perspective enough to accept a work dealing with the customs and traditions of a people who form a comparatively small part of the great aggregation of nationalities having settled in this country? To be sure, the subject in the minds of many publishers was too specialized to interest a general public.

During the summer of 1963 the manuscript came to the attention of Mr. Gerald R. Dillon of Dillon Press, Inc., and later in the year was accepted for publication.

The credit for interesting Mr. Dillon in the manuscript, and for convincing him that Minnesota alone must hold within its borders enough Americans of Swedish descent interested in their cultural heritage to buy up a whole edition, goes to Miss Audrey June Booth, program supervisor, radio station KUOM at the University of Minnesota. For her unceasing encouragement and loyal support throughout I want to express to Miss Booth my warmest appreciation. And my very special thanks to her for the important role she played in getting this book published. I am deeply indebted to her.

Finally, I want to extend to my many loyal friends at the American Swedish Institute in Minneapolis my sincere appreciation for their expressions of good will. The director and staff of the Institute, its Board of Trustees, and the Board of the Swedish Society have both officially and individually done much for the promotion of my book. I thank each and every one warmly.

# BIBLIOGRAPHY

With each nation there is a cultural background that is part of every person born into it. Having been born into the traditions of Sweden, I cannot always tell whether my concepts and attitudes are derived from recollections and observances of earlier days, or whether they are acquired through books. What I have gathered in this book is a blend of both, I think, with personal memories in predominance.

I have, naturally, profited much by extensive reading on the subject and while there may be a number of books in Swedish on traditions and customs that I have not consulted, the following list comprises those from which I gained much information. Other books that were helpful to me are mentioned in the text.

Askeberg, Fritz, and Bengt Holmberg, *Nusvenska*, 1951.
Brobeck, Florence, and Monica Kjellberg, *Scandinavian Cookery for Americans*, 1948.
Brodin, Knut, *Rim och ramsor*, 1937.
Eskeröd, Albert, *Årets fester*, 1953.
Eskeröd, Albert, *Swedish Folk Art Past and Present*, 1961.
Forsberg, Vera, *Majstång och julgran*, 1953.
Gamby, Erik, "Rim och ramsor," *Värld och vetande*, No. 6, 1961.
Heilborn, Adèle, *Travel, Study, and Research*, 1957.

Holm, Pelle, *Bevingade ord,* 1951.

Löfstedt, Annie, and Barbro Svinhufvud, *Min skatt-kammare,* 1959.

Nilsson, Martin P-n, *Festdagar och vardagar,* 1925.

Nilsson, Martin P-n, *Årets folkliga fester,* 1936.

Rasmusson, Ludvig, and Svante Svärdström, *Rikets vapen och flagga,* 1960.

Sundbärg, Gustav, *Det svenska folklynnet,* 1911.

Svärdström, Svante, *Masterpieces of Dala Peasant Paintings,* 1957.

Topelius, Christer, *En bok om julen,* 1960.

# ABOUT THE AUTHOR

Lilly Lorénzen, born and educated in Sweden, came to the United States as a young woman to join her family who had settled earlier in Superior, Wisconsin. For several years she was associate editor of *Kvinnan och Hemmet (Woman and Home)*, at the time the only Swedish woman's magazine in America. After moving to Minneapolis in 1940, she served as executive secretary of the American Swedish Institute until 1948. While there, she began teaching classes in Swedish. During World War II, she taught Swedish to servicemen enrolled in the Army Specialized Training Program at the University of Minnesota, where later she held the position of Instructor in Swedish in the Department of Scandinavian from 1945 to 1961. In the summer of 1947 she conducted the first SPAN (Student Project for Amity among Nations) study tour to Sweden.

Lilly Lorénzen wrote numerous articles and poems, both in English and in Swedish. She also prepared two language courses for the Correspondence Study Department of the University of Minnesota. Script writing for a Twin Cities radio station led to her own program, and as "Ingrid" she entertained her listeners with a program of Scandinavian music and her own lively comments.

In 1963, Lilly Lorénzen was presented with a merit award from Sweden's Tourist Traffic Association in Stockholm for her continuous efforts in promoting greater knowledge and understanding of her homeland in this country. In 1967, His Majesty, the King of Sweden appointed her a member of the Royal Swedish Order of Vasa, First Class.

In this book, dealing with traditions and customs of her native Sweden, Lilly Lorénzen invites the reader to share in her cultural birthright.